Take Flight & Thrive

It's Time to Break Free,

Reclaim Your Worth, and

Soar Higher

Linette Davis

Linette Davis Publishing™
Take Flight & Thrive
© By Linette Davis

All rights reserved. No portion of this may be used or reproduced in any manner whatsoever without written permission from the author and publisher.

ISBN: 978-1-967679-35-5

For details about Speaking Engagements contact us at:

Attn: Linette Davis
Email: info@bellalayor.com
Website: www.BellaLayor.com
Library of Congress Control Number: 2025907997

Table of Contents

Dedication .... **III**
About the Author .... **IV**
Prologue **6**
Introduction **11**
Quadrant 1 Clear the Runway **14**
   Flight Segment 1 Clearing The Runway: No Longer Restricted 32
   Flight Segment 2 35
   Flight Segment 3 38
   Flight Segment 4 Cargo: Baggage Is A Choice 40
   Flight Segment 5 (Part 1) Exceeding Your Allowance: Dealing With Excess Baggage 43
   Flight Segment 5 (Part 2) Traveling Light: Let it go! 44
   Flight Segment 6 Baggage Screening (Checkpoint) 46
   Flight Segment 7 What Are You Using Your Hands For? .. 47
   Flight Segment 8 TSA: Transformational Shift Ahead 49
   Flight Segment 9 Faith and Vision 52
   Flight Segment 10 The Art Of Airporting: Masterfully Navigating With Intention 54
   Flight Segment 11 Aviophobia 58
   Flight Segment 12 The Control Tower: God Is In Control .. 61
   Flight Segment 13 "Prepare for Takeoff…" 64

Quadrant 2 Take Flight **67**
   Flight Segment 14 On The Tarmac 83
   Flight Segment 15 P&R 87
   Flight Segment 16 Get off the Roller Coaster 89
   Flight Segment 17 V1 92
   Flight Segment 18 Lift off to Your Next Level 94
   Flight Segment 19 Wheels Up 97
   Flight Segment 20 Dynamics that Simulate Growth 100
   Flight Segment 21 Air Traffic Control 102
   Flight Segment 22 Bird Strikes 103
   Flight Segment 23 Airplane Mode 104
   Flight Segment 24 Altitude 105
   Flight Segment 25 Cloud 9 108

    Flight Segment 26 GO 109

Quadrant 3 Soar 111
    Flight Segment 27 Air Pressure Changes 138
    Flight Segment 28 Storms of Life 141
    Flight Segment 29 Thrive Through Turbulence 142
    Flight Segment 30 Just Wing It 146
    Flight Segment 31 On the Fly 151
    Flight Segment 32 Tailwind 152
    Flight Segment 33 Hijacked 155
    Flight Segment 34 Layovers 157
    Flight Segment 35 Fear Factor 159
    Flight Segment 36 Pardon Me 163
    Flight Segment 37 Precious Cargo Onboard 165
    Flight Segment 38 Flying First Class 167
    Flight Segment 39 N.E.S.W 169

QUAD 4 171
Landing On Purpose 171
    Flight Segment 40 Longevity For The Long Haul 188
    Flight Segment 41 Inner First-Class Experience 190
    Flight Segment 42 Vertical Vantage 192
    Flight Segment 43 Expectations & Encounters 194
    Flight Segment 44 Operating Cost 196
    Flight Segment 45 No Smoking Inside The Cabin 198
    Flight Segment 46 Positioned To Prevail 200
    Flight Segment 47 Understanding Your Airworthiness Through Grace 202
    Flight Segment 48 Return On Investment 204
    Flight Segment 49 Passport Power 206
    Flight Segment 50 Only God Could Have Orchestrated This 208
    Flight Segment 51 Stand by: Ready to be Used by God 210
    Flight Segment 52 Expand Your Vision Worldwide 212

Disclaimer

The resources listed in this guide are not intended to be fully systematic or complete, nor does inclusion here imply any endorsement or recommendation by Linette Davis, Curtis Publishing. Linette Davis, Curtis Publishing, make no warranties, expressed or implied, about the value or utility of any purpose of the information and resources contained herein.

Clear the Runway

"But now, this is what the Lord says... Fear not, for I have redeemed you; I have summoned you by name; you are mine."

—Isaiah 43:1

My Grace is sufficient for you, for my power is made perfect in weakness."

—2 Corinthians 12:9

Take Flight

"Have I not commanded you? Be strong and courageous. Do not be terrified; do not be discouraged, for the Lord your God will be with you wherever you go."

—Joshua 1:9

Soar

"Humble yourselves, then, under God's mighty hand, so that he will lift you up in his own good time. Leave all your worries with him, because he cares for you."

—1 Peter 5:6-7

Landing on purpose

"For I know the plans I have for you," declares the LORD, "plans to prosper you and not to harm you, plans to give you hope and a future."

—Jeremiah 29:11

Dedication

To my daughter Layor Exousia Harris and my son Amani Jabari Harris

♥

Be Brave. Never take life for granted.

♥

Pray & Live courageously, Every. Single. Day. Choose to be fearless as you go humbly, step by step.

♥

Take moments to be still and reflect.

♥

Travel often and never let anyone stop your laughter.

♥

Be kind but not vulnerable to those who take advantage. Give and receive and let your heart be full.

♥

Show the same grace to others as God has shown you.

♥

Set the standard and leave a lasting legacy.

♥

Be *Yourself* and know who you are and also who you are growing to be. Be the one and only. Excellence is in your DNA, so with all that you are and all that you do, shine with excellence.

♥

Love fully and never be brokenhearted for too long.

♥

Never give up and never lose faith.

♥

Hope is yours always—to hold onto and to share with others.

♥

Nothing is impossible for you, my love. I love you now and forever.

About the Author

As Linette Davis is the definition of resilient, the CEO and founder of Bella Layor LLC and Trauma to Transformation non-profit, she has created multiple platforms to inspire women around the world to heal, rebuild, and transform their lives.

Linette's life mission exudes passion and love for igniting hope, resiliency, and empowerment. Majority of her career has been spent helping children and women overcome abuse, sexual trauma, and life's misfortunes. Linette has advocated for and counseled thousands of individuals, including women, men, teens, and children.

Additionally, she has conducted workshops, master classes, and speaking engagements revolving around empowerment, self-esteem, vision boards, emotional health, inner resiliency, and corporate resiliency in the workplace. She is also a published author of "Metaphors for Healing, Rebuilding, and Transforming Your Life into a Beautiful Warrior," a book to help you navigate life and the pains of life so you can live in the freedom God has for you!

She hopes that her work will inspire you to take flight and live out your God-given purpose! She knows the words in this book will shift you back into alignment and accelerate the changes that are necessary for you in this season. She prays you to gain momentum as you travel through the quadrants of this book on your way to a deeper sense of freedom. She believes that your best life is ahead as long as you commit to doing the work and keeping your focus full speed ahead.

Prologue

One of my favorite things to do is fly! One early morning I was eagerly anticipating my flight from Orlando International Airport (MCO) to Atlanta's Hartsfield Airport (ATL). I was dropped off at the departure section, and cool, crisp air welcomed me as I entered the double sliding doors that whisk you quickly into a world of its own.

A Transportation Security Administration (TSA) pre-check security agent allowed me to check into the wrong terminal. Neither one of us paid any attention to the gate or the terminal. Clearly, Delta was not in her terminal but my barcode scanned and lit up green for access. But access to where? I was granted access to a terminal with several planes, but not a single one was the designated plane for me that day. Delta was on the other side of the airport and I found myself on the opposite end. I walked off the tram, looked at my watch and was proud to have 1 minute before boarding. It was exactly 7:39 a.m. I let out a sigh of relief I was on time, not too early and not too late. I was committed to being on time this year. Plus I was cute, full-on makeup, and I had my newest Ted Baker suitcase in hand. I was giving myself an imaginary pat on the back. In the next moment, I saw 1-29, 30-49, 50-69; it dawned on me that I had no idea what gate number I was assigned so I checked my Delta app. I noticed it said 89; I quickly re-glanced as if the number 89 was going to magically appear. I walked up to the screen and didn't even see Delta on the screen for departing flights or arrivals.

You know that feeling of dread that takes over when you find yourself in a place where your expectations were not fulfilled, a place you thought would bring you a promised outcome, but you found yourself lost instead. You thought it would be a place of belonging, but you ended up where you didn't belong. I was there. In a moment's time, my "on time" switched to "not enough time." I ran to the first attendant, asking and confirming at the same time, "Delta isn't here, is it?"

He replied, "It's on the other end of the airport."

Then he asked, "What time is your boarding?"

I said, "They are boarding now!"

He said, "You won't make it!"

I didn't confirm what he said; I just turned around and ran towards the next tram back. I had to wait though, as one just took off from the platform. It sunk in, I had not paid attention. I was aimlessly following the crowd through terminal B, which I have travelled several times. But I wasn't supposed to travel here today (or was I?). With a dozen roses, passport and luggage in hand, I bolted to the other side of the airport. An unexpected cardio workout taking place without my planning.

I am the type of person who, when someone tells me I can't do it, I prove them wrong; at least I'll try my darndest. I ran to terminal A's security counter, checked in, navigated through security, and jumped onto another tram. An older gentleman asked, "Where are you heading?"

I told him, "I'm finally heading in the right direction after going to the wrong terminal."

He asked, "What time my flight was and I told him 8:20 a.m."

He replied, "You can make it!" Then he complimented me, saying that I smelled good. I thanked him and smiled. Little did he know that I was really thanking him for the confirmation, not the compliment. I stood up as the tram slowed, and he said you will make it and let that set the tone for your day! I smiled and peeled through the small opening as the tram glass doors slid open. I ran again, this time down the lengthy terminal to Delta.

The first guy was right; it was on the other end and my gate 89 was the very last one. But the second guy was right, I made it!

I heard the last call before the gate closed for flight 2205. I was sweating but still smelling good. Ted Baker fully travelled at this point and flowers in hand.

What others saw as a for-sure error that couldn't be overcome, I chose to believe in something else.

When they wrote me off, based on their perceptions of distance, time, and probability, I chose to believe in something else.

It didn't matter what they determined. I chose to defy the odds and take flight to my flight! I could have given up and went back to ticketing with lost hope and minimal chance of getting to where I needed to be that day with more expense and a huge loss of time, but I chose to PUSH! When I didn't confirm the negative spoken to me, the next person I spoke with confirmed the positive belief I set in motion! See how that works?

The only thing that mattered was me getting where I needed to be as fast as humanly possible so I can get where I needed to go!

That was all that mattered to me!

And all that should matter to you!

Take the world by flight with your God-given purpose! You are not out of time; it's your time! You were made to move mountains and defy the odds!

Find a way or make a way with no apologies! Grace is on your side, so go for it and take flight!

```
G   R   A   C   E
R       is      G
A       on      R
C      your     A
E      side     C
G   R   A   C   E
```

Introduction

Most people love to travel, or at least most people like the concept of travelling. It's not often that people stop to reflect on the actual process of travelling. I know personally that I love going somewhere new and adventurous, but I despise the point in travel when my shoulders feel like bricks because I've overpacked. I love that flights are quicker, but the risk can seem higher. I love that travelling is a physical, mental, and spiritual journey for me. I hate that so many miss the treasures in taking flight and the keys to taking flight in their own lives. That's why I wrote this book as a tool to empower you to be intentional about living God's best for your life! This book challenges you to level up and take flight with each personalized analogy geared to stimulate new dimensions of your life. This will be your passport to a new destiny.

Taking flight from one destination to another, first, requires a decision. A decision to leave where you are and go to a new place, a decision that has to be backed up by your actions and several more actions and decisions that follow. Taking a flight requires you to pay for your ticket and begin preparing for the journey ahead.

Much of this book was written and developed while sitting in the Orlando International Airport (MCO). I have observed families experiencing their first trip together, carts filled with suitcases and kids jumping through the design of the colored carpets as their parents eagerly search for signs to get to their flight. I have witnessed the calm and the rushed alike, contending through the multitude to beat the countdown of time. I have witnessed the hugs and kisses between two people that establish separation, leaving two trails of tears in opposite directions. I have heard the breaths of many who were out of breath and equally the complaints and joys spoken about their experience in the airport. I have smelled the rubbery metal of baggage claim mixed with the thick air that follows well-flighted people; I have also smelled the sweet aroma of coffee and cinnamon buns as I have walked throughout the airport. I have seen the faces of those who ran as fast as they could to their gate, only to realize that they still missed their flight. I have seen the havoc the security process can have on a person's affect as well as the kindness of a flight attendant. But, what I have seen most are people like you and I, journeying throughout life the best they can, coping, healing, relating, and un-relating, sometimes aimlessly and sometimes intentionally, being and becoming, growing, evolving, and changing, through moments of time, as they experience reality, but hope for a transformation.

Quadrant 1
Clear the Runway

"But now, this is what the Lord says… Fear not, for I have redeemed you; I have summoned you by name; you are mine."

—Isaiah 43:1

"My Grace is sufficient for you, for my power is made perfect in weakness."

—2 Corinthians 12:9

"If you want to fly you have to give up the "stuff" that weighs you down."

—Toni Morrison

Clear the Runway

Has God placed a dream or a vision inside you? Many times, you may sense a divine uneasiness that won't let you rest or settle until you do something about it. Your life may not resemble the great future and plan God has for you now – however, when you commit, from this day forward, to remove the obstacles, take a step of F

$$A$$

$$I$$

$$T$$

$$H$$

F O R W A R D and prepare yourself—you draw closer to God's plan for your life.

The good news is that God has already placed His purpose within you. You are chosen, you are called, you are redeemed. So now, let's take this time to get connected with God on a deeper level so you can clear the runway in preparation to take flight so you can move higher and closer than you've ever been to your destiny.

S	W	A	Y	N
O	H	R	O	O
	E	E	U	W?
	R			
	E			

Do you know where planes are kept when they are not in use?

Planes are kept in what is called a hangar. The hangar is only a temporary, I repeat: temporary, place of protection for rest and repair.

What Kind of Hangar

|	|
|	|
|	|
|	|

Are you currently in?

A hangar of doubt, financial burden, busyness, pride, a hangar of the past? A hangar of indecision and inaction? Perhaps you've been in a hangar of grief, broken-heartedness, impulsivity, a hangar lacking faith and freedom, a hanger of complacency, laziness or overwhelm? There are hangers of anxiety, stress, burnout, routine, and instability.

You may be experiencing a generational hangar from your childhood. Perhaps you chose to stay because you desired the comfort of familiarity.

You may be in a hanger of past accomplishments and achievements, yet never experiencing deep fulfillment. Many people settle here, in the hangar. They settle for what they see, what they feel, what they have been told, and they settle for what they have been through. Don't settle for a hangar when you were

   B
      O
         R
            N
               To
                     F
                        L
                          Y!

Now is the time to leave behind the place of comfort and complacency. God is positioning you to walk out the vision He has for your life. DO NOT STAY WHERE YOU ARE! Today, refuse to settle for the hangar.

You must recognize and understand that there is MORE to life than where you presently are. There is MORE purpose, MORE blessings, MORE joy and increasingly MORE grace. As you live out God's will for your life, the MORE you will experience your best life.

I know you want to experience life outside of the hangar, and now that you know where you are, it's time to commit to moving out of that hangar and away from the fruitless settings that keep you complacent.

It is common knowledge that planes don't back right out onto the runway and take off immediately. There are several turns that need to be made, in just the right order, in order for you to get to the right position on the runway so you are given the green light for take off. It's all about...

POSITIONING

Positioning is everything. Some people may get impatient and frustrated. Some people even give up, not realizing that they are one to two turns away from being in the right position to take flight. Some even feel lost or feel like they've been abandoned, but they're simply one turn away from taking flight.

You can't let anything hinder you from taking flight—not even impatience. You must have the diligence, the discipline, the tenacity, the perseverance and the commitment to take flight. You must know that the destination will be well worth the journey and everything you had to go through in order to get there.

It's time you "lay aside every weight" to take flight and live the life God intended for you. God has plans for you to

        O

S

                R!

       A

So how do you get from where you are now to the skies? The first step is to commit to the introspective and transformational process ahead. There are many roadblocks and also many things that you want to attach to your life as baggage, but you will be better off if you leave those things behind, position yourself on the runway, and prepare to take flight.

The runway is an appointed place where God has created for you to take flight. The runway is a unique territory, built to hold weight and built long in length to give way for speed and altitude. Spiritually, runways are constructed of grace and grit but in reality, runways are constructed with gravel to hold almost one million pounds. They are constructed to accommodate a variety of airplanes in size and weight, a variety of temperatures, a variety of wind velocities, and a variety of conditions. A solid runway is designed to prevent the ground from cracking and buckling under the pressure of takeoff and landing. The runway is not miles wide; it's narrow. You have to stay in your lane and you have to stay focused.

There is a designated pathway for you to move, which means your positioning must be just right.

The right positioning happens through diligent prayer, reflection, good counsel and the leading of the Holy Spirit. You must make daily decisions to step into your divine birthright—your place to take flight.

You may have what you need. You may be positioned... however, you are not yet ready for takeoff. First, you must

> CLEAR
>
> THE
>
> RUNWAY.

You have no more room to harbor negative thoughts and patterns of bondage. There is a new level of freedom where God wants to take you. Yet, you must let go in order to experience that new level God has for you.

Clearing the runway means clearing your mind, your time, your heart, your energy, your responsibilities and all your "ish" so you can focus fully on your God-given purpose. Take some time to think about the mindsets, attitudes, thoughts and behaviors that have governed your life and/or recent circumstances.

It's time to take a long, hard look at what you bring with you to your destination. The space you have is limited, so what you allow into your space matters.

Many times, we hold on to stories in our lives that aren't bearing any fruit or producing any growth or progress in our lives. Instead, these thoughts and beliefs are taking up space that's designed to be fruitful and produce a harvest in our lives. What fruitless things are occupying a fruitful space?

Clearing the runway means REMOVING ANY & ALL RESTRICTIONS to continued movement!

If we are going to take flight, we must be very INTENTIONAL about our: TIME, ENERGY, HEALTH, EMOTIONS, PURPOSE, MENTAL HEALTH, WELLBEING, RELATIONSHIPS, & DECISIONS!

Time can be drained in procrastination, when we are not purpose-minded about who we are and what we will and will not do.

Where is your time going?

What issues are soaking up your energy?

Are there relationships that strain you mentally and emotionally?

What are you carrying with you from childhood, from adolescence, from past relationships or disappointments?

Observe the old patterns that exist in your life that are producing things you don't want in your life – ~~unhappiness, fear, doubt, sadness, depression, anxiety~~ and the list goes on. Instead of bringing value to your flight and helping you reach your destination, this extra baggage can

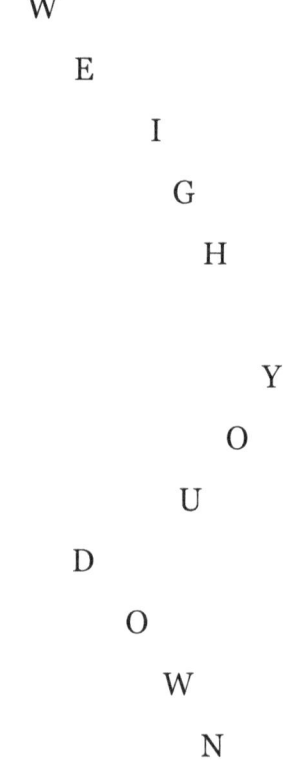

& diminish the quality of your flight.

You must consider what you will need for your destination. Will you need wisdom? (Yes.) Will you need peace of mind?

(Yes.) Will you need an abundance mindset? (Yes.) Know that some baggage can be positive and some negative. If you carry along negative, energy-sapping emotions of fear, guilt, shame and insecurity, it will weigh you down. Plus, when you get to your destination—you'll still have those self-sabotaging mindsets—even when you arrive at your new place of destiny.

The emotional, mental and spiritual luggage you "carry on" will go on to impact not only yourself, but many others. Baggage happens, but you must consider how much weight you choose to carry with you. The truth is—it's hard work carrying around negative emotional and mental baggage.

Imagine filling your suitcases with big, heavy rocks. It would be such a burdensome task. You would have to work so hard to carry those things around wherever you desired to go.

No one would want to carry it to the bathroom, to a restaurant, to work, inside your family's home when you visit and lug it back to your car, pack it up, bring it home, shower with it, cook with it on your shoulders, and then go to sleep in bed with it.

This is what we do when we harbor past emotions and memories fresh in our hearts and minds. This is what we do when we hold on to untrue stories about who we are, or the negative things people may have said about us.

When you find yourself holding onto those things, picture yourself, metaphorically, lugging around those heavy suitcases filled with rocks. This emotional baggage keeps relationships and opportunities at a distance. No one can get too close. We pad our hearts and minds, our emotions, our mental space and the intimate spaces we hold with others with dead weight.

Anger, unforgiveness, and resentment can absorb your vitality and sense of purpose. One heated discussion, one rage-filled memory, can delay you from getting to your destination.

The same dead weight that can keep us from letting others in can keep us from letting God into our hearts. Independence and self-reliance are applauded in our generation. It can be easy to turn within oneself and stop trusting in others—and even stop trusting in God when you have been disappointed. You must find a way, however to trust God with your life, your heart, and your emotions and recognize that you need God in order to take flight.

God has an arsenal of peace, love, joy and beautiful things for you to share with the world. You owe it to God, who gives good gifts, to live out your purpose and give to the world those beautiful things He has given you access to. Be the person who gives hope, joy, and the things God intended you to give. Don't allow sadness, depression, bitterness, loneliness, betrayal and other things to steal away your purpose, your joy and the legacy of love God intended for your life.

God is the Control Tower. He has the Master Flight Plan. So even if you need to be redirected back to the terminal to drop off some dead weight, even if your position on the runway isn't as glamorous as you thought it would be, even if you need to sit in the hangar for a while longer or get out of the hangar and get moving

—God is there guiding you

T

H

EVERY

TRANSITION

U

G

H

Let that sink in, I said, God is there with you, through every transition. We won't make it to the destiny God has for us without being fully connected and obedient to His plan.

Aren't you tired of your plan? Your way?

"Come to me, all you who are weary and burdened, and I will give you rest." Matthew 11:28 (NIV)

God has a space for you to be happy, whole and complete. Once movement begins, you will be on your way. The speed required for takeoff will be so fast, there will be no time to stop for distractions, obstacles and hindrances. However, when you are upset and harboring negativity within your spirit, the energy that would be used to fuel your takeoff will be used to weigh you down.

Enough is enough. There is a flight scheduled in your life. You have a destination, a purpose, and a meaningful assignment over your life. God wants to connect with you—to usher you into a place of bliss and glory. It's the destination He has intended, specially for you. Your gifts, your experience, your skill sets and your talents are the perfect fit for where God wants you to go.

However, this new place requires a paradigm shift in order for you to fully appreciate the promises that you will realize once you arrive at your destination.

Old mindsets must go. We must release pride, fear, shame and the past, knowing and understanding that God has a place of rest for us. No longer do we need to carry the heavy load of emotional baggage that slows us down and keeps us rooted in depression and unnecessary pain. We can accelerate our process by surrendering to God's plan. We can move forward quicker and in a more powerful way, when we let go of what we have and free up our lives to receive what God has for us.

Are you ready to receive God's fullness? If our hands are filled with past stories, guilt, shame, fear and anger—we are too full of ourselves to receive His fullness. We must make room. We must clear the runway.

Confront the things you've struggled with but you've never told a soul. Go ahead, acknowledge the things you've never acknowledged to God.

Some people have been victimized and never acknowledged it. Some have been utterly rebellious to the point they question if grace exists for them, some broken and without hope - hurting to the point of questioning life itself. Now is the time to acknowledge it so you can heal, overcome, and reclaim your God-given identity, your God-given purpose, your God-given power!

```
                    C
                    O
                    N
     Anything       F     Everything
                    R
                    O
                   AND
                    T
```

...that represents baggage, negative patterns, generational cycles, depressive thought cycles and triggers, and even emotional spending habits and mental self-sabotage. Confront anything that represents a weight, or extra baggage, that slowing you down and keeping your life from fully taking flight.

It's time to clear the runway once and for all.

There are two kinds of hangars, positive and negative. A positive hangar would be a hangar for a time of deep healing and isolation with God. A negative hangar would be choosing to live in fear over being obedient to God's purpose in your life. Nevertheless, hangars are built to be TEMPORARY resting places for planes, not permanent residences. Planes are meant to be in the air, just like you and I are meant to SOAR!

Don't take up permanent residence in a temporary relationship or circumstantial pain.

What kind of hangar are you currently in?

Flight Segment 1
Clearing The Runway: No Longer Restricted

When we remove barriers in our lives, we are not only finding our way back to our true selves but we are also committing to see beyond our current circumstances. Many experience extended times when they can't see beyond their circumstance, and their faith grows exhausted. We often get frustrated, not realizing that we have the power to remove the residue of life that is keeping us stuck. We have the power to navigate around opposition. We have the power to make better decisions and reposition our position. Doing this allows us to live unrestricted, unblocked and unstuck. When we clear the runway of our lives, it energizes our faith.

Clear (adjective): to see easily, unclouded, transparent, user-friendly, simple,

Clear (adverb): completely, thoroughly, fully, wholly, entirely,

Clear (verb): to remove an obstruction or unwanted item, to free, to rid, to strip, to unburden, to unblock, to unclog, to move, to shift, to unstop, to do away with, to ditch, to eliminate,

What comes to mind when you read the words, "Clear the runway?'

What needs to be cleared from your life in order for you to take flight?

Remember, nothing changes if nothing changes!

FACT: Most commercial airport runways are typically 2 to 4 feet thick with layers of asphalt.

As stated, your runway is a unique territory, a strategic place for you to shift! This shift/movement that is necessary for you also requires you to have a solid foundation. For me, overcoming childhood sexual trauma, emotional trauma, and mental abuse set a strong foundation of grace, redemption and freedom. Now, the dirt and horrible experiences made to break me are the same experiences now covered in grace made to propel me!

Run: to move with speed, fail to stop, bolt, take flight, clear out, go through, to make a break for it, to advance, flow, to go in a particular direction.

Way: a process, a strategy, a route, a plan, a system, a position, a track, a path, a journey, a particular area, parts in which something divides or is divided

What is the foundation of your runway?

"Progress is impossible without change, and those who cannot change their minds cannot change anything."

—George Bernard Shaw

Flight Segment 2
<u>More</u>

It doesn't **M**atter where y**O**u a**RE** or what you have done or haven't done, your life can be transfor**M**ed with G**O**d's g**R**ac**E**.

THERE IS SOMETHING

M (MILLIONS)

O (OVERFLOW)

R (REDEMPTION)

E (EXPANSION)

FOR YOU!

Is it a passion yet to be ignited, a purpose currently un**F**ulfilled, **OR** a dream yet to be lived? God doesn't want **YOU** to live your life in vain when he has **F**illed y**O**u with pu**R**pose and given **YOU** the ultimate gift of life.

Today, God is calling you to more! Something major, something orchestrated just for you, something right now, and something everlasting!

Today, God is calling you to live your best life!

<u>Ephesians 1:1-14 (NIV)</u>

Paul, an apostle of Christ Jesus by the will of God, to God's holy people in Ephesus, the faithful in Christ Jesus: Grace and peace to you from God our Father and the Lord Jesus Christ. Praise be to the God and Father of our Lord Jesus Christ, who has blessed us in the heavenly realms with every spiritual blessing in Christ. For he chose us in him before the creation of the world to be holy and blameless in his sight.

In love, he predestined us for adoption to sonship through Jesus Christ, in accordance with his pleasure and will—to the praise of his glorious grace, which he has freely given us in the One he loves. In him, we have redemption through his blood, the forgiveness of sins, in accordance with the riches of God's grace that he lavished on us. With all wisdom and understanding, he made known to us the mystery of his will according to his good pleasure, which he purposed in Christ, to be put into effect when the times reach their fulfillment—to bring unity to all things in heaven and on earth under Christ.

In him we were also chosen, having been predestined according to the plan of him who works out everything in conformity with the purpose of his will, in order that we, who were the first to put our hope in Christ, might be for the praise of his glory. And you also were included in Christ when you heard the message of truth, the gospel of your salvation. When you believed, you were marked in him with a seal, the promised Holy Spirit, who is a deposit guaranteeing our inheritance until the redemption of those who are God's possession—to the praise of his glory.

Flight Segment 3
<u>Your Best Life</u>

Your best life doesn't coincide with your emotions.
Your best life doesn't coincide with your flesh.
Your best life doesn't coincide with your will for self.
Your best life doesn't coincide with others will for your life.
Your best life doesn't coincide within your comfort zone.

Your best life coincides with your obedience to God's directives!

Your best life coincides when you operate in God's grace!
Your best life coincides with your yes to surrender to God!
Your best life coincides when your faith in God rings louder than your fears.

Verse
Philippians 4:6 (NIV)
Do not be anxious about anything, but in every situation, by prayer and petition, with thanksgiving, present your request to God.

This verse instructs us to confidently make our request known to God. God desires for you to come to Him with your praise, with your needs and your requests. Your prayers are heard and your prayers are important to God. Did you know it makes God happy to answer our prayers? Pray for clarity for the vision of God's best for your life.

Flight Segment 4
Cargo: Baggage Is A Choice

Now that you have connected to the vision of God's best for your life, it's time to prepare for the flight to your destiny. It's usually from the comfort of our homes that we need to decipher through what we have, what we need, and what we determine will be useful upon arrival to our new destination. The items in the comforts of our home are not perceived as baggage until we pack up and journey to a new destination. There are things in your possession that you do not feel the weight of, until you leave a place of familiarity. For example, the items in your home occupy space. You typically do not realize how many items (and junk) you have until you move to a new home. During a move the items once deemed a normality of a past situation now turn into baggage. When we level up in life, it forces us to evaluate the habits, ways, and patterns that operate in our life. It forces us to confront the thoughts and emotions driving our actions as well as the actions driving our thoughts and emotions.

Now, we will confront the baggage of life so that you aren't weighed down at the new level God is taking you.

Life can be tough!

___ ___ ___ ___ ___ ___

Along the way, you may have been given baggage, you may have picked up baggage, or you have allowed baggage into your life. No one ever wants baggage, but we all deal with it in some way. Baggage is a burden that can be hard to carry forward. Baggage affects your core and your fundamental belief system. Your core is your mind, heart, and soul. It's the way you perceive yourself and the way you view God, which in turn impacts your faith. Baggage influences your relationships. Baggage impacts your level of fulfillment in life.

What baggage is currently in your life?

What weighs you down?

Quote

"Just because you have baggage doesn't mean you have to lug it around."

—Richie Norton

Fact: The average suitcase weighs about 30 kilograms, which is just under 70 lbs.

Think of the baggage in your current life. Metaphorically, what does it look like, and how much does it weigh?

Reflection: When personal luggage exceeds a maximum allowance, the individual is charged a fee. The baggage in your life will cost you! What has it already cost you? What will it cost you if you don't deal with it today?

Flight Segment 5 (Part 1)
<u>Exceeding Your Allowance: Dealing With Excess Baggage</u>

Baggage can be a challenge to face; it's not an easy task. The best way to deal with baggage is with truth, fully and completely. Don't just deal with some of it; deal with all of it now so it doesn't show up in your future.

"You should carry with you the things you need during the flight, and at your final destination. Do not carry with you excess baggage."

Linette Davis

Do not continue to take unnecessary baggage into your future.

Be brave

      and

            Be honest with yourself!

Choose to let go of unnecessary baggage in order to gain a powerful step forward towards your destiny.

Flight Segment 5 (Part 2)
Traveling Light: Let it go!

Let go of painful memories.

E

T

G

O

Let go of hurtful experiences.

E

T

G

O

Let go of the lies.

E

T

G

O

Let go of the ill will others spoke over your life.

LET IT ALL GO!

You won't need it and truthfully, you don't want it. Choose peace. No hoarding the past. You need space for freedom to exist.

Letting go allows you to be open to receive.

Did you know that the things you have not forgiven yourself for are also baggage? What things have you not forgiven yourself for? What mistakes serve as a constant redirection from your purpose and value in Christ?

What regrets do you need to release from your life?

Flight Segment 6
Baggage Screening (Checkpoint)

Thousands of bags get checked in at the airport. Those bags go through intensive baggage screening systems, subsystems, and routes to get to their destination. Each airport has primary conveyor belts that branch out to multiple airline stations to transport passenger bags.

When was the last time you thoroughly inspected your baggage for dangerous items that you have held onto?

I remember borrowing my father's suitcase for a trip and I was stopped by TSA for having multiple tools in the front pocket of the suitcase. I wasn't even aware that those items were there until I was screened!

The baggage system and route is very complex; the complexity of this system is monitored and maintained by the TSA (Transportation Security Administration) to ensure the safety of each bag.

When we go through life without yielding to the Holy Spirit, our internal TSA is weakened, allowing prohibited items to pass our checkpoints, missed suspicious activity, and hazardous materials into our hearts and minds.

Flight Segment 7
What Are You Using Your Hands For?

If you go to any airport and observe, you will notice that baggage usually occupies people's hands. Hands are a very important part of the human body. Hands are used for grasping things, holding things, and moving things. Hands are used for work. Hands are also used for greeting others with hellos and goodbyes. Hands also illustrate our ability to give and receive.

Is baggage inhibiting you from extending and receiving help and blessings? Many people are holding onto the baggage of life so much that if a blessing were to come their way they would not be able to receive it. You cannot receive anything new if you stay consumed by the baggage you are currently holding onto.

Imagine walking in an airport, lugging around multiple suitcases. Your muscles are tired and you still have a distance ahead to get to your gate. If someone were to approach you and tell you that they were gifting you with an extra large box of tissue in exchange for your baggage, you would probably not see the value in the gift. More than likely, since your hands and space were already occupied with things you determined were more valuable than the box of tissue, you would likely continue your path without releasing your grip on your baggage in exchange for the box.

In the same scenario, if a person showed you that the box was filled with a million dollars, you would likely decide that you will release what is in your hands in anticipation of something you deemed more valuable than what you currently possessed. You will need to decide that what is being offered to you is of greater value than what you are holding onto! I can assure you this: your past is not worth holding onto! God has so much more for you!

Are you ready to release what you are holding onto in exchange for the life God intended for you to live?

The unnecessary baggage you take with you will not only cost you something, but it will cost those around you something as well. Are your children paying the price of your baggage? Is your spouse paying the price of your baggage? Is your marriage taxed as a result of your baggage? Are your friends paying the price of your baggage? Who else is paying the price of your baggage?

Flight Segment 8
TSA: Transformational Shift Ahead

You must create space for transformation to happen! God needs space in your life. He needs you to make room so he can pour into your life and expand your capacity for grace and purpose.

The baggage we carry attaches itself to our physical bodies and our mental space!

The baggage we carry attaches itself to our energy!

The baggage we carry attaches itself to the speed at which we move!

The baggage we carry attaches itself to our future destination!

The baggage we carry is a choice!

Read it again.

The baggage I carry attaches itself to my physical body and my mental space!

The baggage I carry attaches itself to my energy!

The baggage I carry attaches itself to the speed at which I move!

The baggage I carry attaches itself to my future destination!

The baggage I carry is a choice!

List reasons you are committed to releasing the baggage in your current life.

Reason 1

Reason 2

Reason 3

Reason 4

Reason 5

Reason 6

Reason 7

Reason 8

Reason 9

Reason 10

Isaiah 43:18

"Forget the former things; do not dwell on the past."

Flight Segment 9
Faith and Vision

Faith is complete and confident belief, expectation, and trust. Vision is the state of being able to see and also the supernatural ability to see the future in your mind.

There will be times when what you physically see contradicts the thing that you are entrusting to God. Know that this is not your ticket to despair, discouragement, or disobedience (distrust in God). This is an exercise of your faith; the exercise is "complete and confident." Your faith isn't truly stretched unless it's forced against our flesh and what is comfortable.

When we stay in communion with God, what takes place is miraculous. God fills our spirits with His purpose, His peace, and His presence.

Outside of that communion we entrust our own devices, ultimately rooted in pain and pride.

Did you know?

A pilot must have 20/20 vision, with or without corrective lenses, to become a civilian airline pilot.

In short, a pilot must have a clear vision to even qualify. A pilot could have all the skills necessary, but they could be disqualified due to their vision. Could you even imagine depending on pilots and co-pilots with poor vision and foresight? That's incredibly dangerous.

Can you see where you are going?

We must be able to see clearly spiritually! It's a mandate. Your vision must be clear in order to take flight! You must operate from a place of emotional, spiritual, and mental clarity. Is your vision clear? Are you able to see not only the seen but the unseen?

Fact: Did you know that, unlike cars, airplanes are not equipped with rearview mirrors or side mirrors? Many car drivers are accustomed to using side mirrors and rearview mirrors to see the opposite direction of travel and to see behind themselves during a journey forward. One can agree that if a person uses only a side mirror or rear view mirror to travel forward, this would be an accident waiting to happen.

In the same respect, having a perfect vision as you look forward but only seeing the past is also detrimental.

When you take flight in your life, like an airplane, it is not optional for you to focus on the things behind you. In order to get to your destination, you must be forward-thinking. Your daily decisions, habits, thoughts, your focus must all be in alignment with your destiny.

Flight Segment 10
<u>The Art Of Airporting: Masterfully Navigating With Intention</u>

There were several years as a young adult when my travelling experience was more of a fight or flight experience rather than a peaceful, well-planned event. I was the girl one would see unpacking her bags at ticketing because my suitcase was 20lbs heavier than the limit. I was also the girl you would see lugging too many suitcases because I thought I needed the majority of my closet, "just in case." I made most of my flights in the nick of time, and I was proud of that although gut-wrenching, still a thrill. Secretly, I desired to be the woman who somehow packed a perfectly small, organized suitcase and casually strolled through the airport as if she were walking the beach or perhaps the fashion runway, unfazed by all the stress around her that others failed to avoid.

First, I realized that my past experiences were a mirror of my life. I was holding onto things like excuses "just in case," and I was carrying a lot that was only slowing me down. So, I started to take note of the things I truly needed and accepted the challenge that a 19-inch Ted Baker suitcase would bring... simplicity, style and intention from the terminal all the way to the tarmac!

Secondly, I learned that attention and intention are two very, very different experiences. To give attention to something means you've acknowledged its importance. To give something intention means you are giving it purpose and energy, and you are committing to a process.

In life, things draw your attention or you can choose how much attention to give at any given moment. Attention can be lost easily or never given fully. Attention is heavily dependent on stimuli; giving attention may happen consciously or unconsciously.

In life, being intentional means you refuse to be dragged through life day after day, week after week, and month after month. Being intentional means to have a purpose behind your actions and the things you do for the desired outcome you intend to reach.

You don't have to have your entire life mapped out, but you do need to have your values and purpose at the forefront of your mind, ensuring your life on the outside is aligned with your inner world (heart, mind, spirit).

Are you navigating life with attention or intention?

Have you noticed a difference when you are just allowing life to bring your attention to things rather than purposefully navigating life with intention?

Life grabs our attention when things happen, but how often are we truly intentional about our life.

Did you know?

In the United States, 2 million passengers board more than 30,000 flights every day.

About 1 in 5 people have some fear of flying, or "aviophobia."

Flight Segment 11
Aviophobia

Aviophobia is the fear of flying. Although traveling by plane is one of the safest methods of transportation, many fear it because of the unknown, because they are not in control, and because of lack of knowledge, to name a few reasons. I've witnessed people with their paid ticket in hand, baggage already routed to the airplane, and they are stuck just steps away from getting onto the plane due to fear. Fear is paralyzing. Imagine freezing yourself exactly where you are in the moment for a week, no motion or movement at all. What do you think happens when we are afraid to pursue our purpose? What do you think happens when God calls us and we allow fear to immobilize us? Fear is a liar and a thief. Fear will rob you!

What fears are keeping you stuck at the gate?

"When fears are grounded, dreams take flight."

—*Unknown Author*

"I'm not afraid of flying, I'm afraid of not flying."

—Unknown Author

Flight Segment 12
The Control Tower: God Is In Control

Before any flight takes off, a flight plan must be filed with the control tower. A flight plan is the master pilot's intended path to take you, the passenger, to your destination. It includes the altitude, the direction, the route being flown and the direction of travel.

The control tower is a place that holds all of the flight plans for every plane that is preparing for takeoff, in flight, or preparing to land. Well, friends, God is the control tower of our lives. He has the Master Flight Plan (purpose with your name on it)–He understands which route we need to take to get us where we want to be. God knows the speed and the direction that is just right for us.

Jeremiah 29:11 says,

"For I know the plans I have for you," declares the L*ORD*, *"plans to prosper you and not to harm you, plans to give you hope and a future."*

Only a small percentage of the world's population has ever traveled by plane.

Flight Segment 13
"Prepare for Takeoff…"

So perhaps you're in a place where you are ready for things to change. You are looking for a shift. You want to walk in the plans of God, but you're not quite sure how to "take off." Listen, if you want to level up and elevate your potential, you must prepare yourself, from the inside out, to go higher.

God is looking to prepare you, to make you stronger mentally and emotionally, to increase your finances, to develop your mindset, to strengthen and detoxify your relationships. All these things must take place in order to get you in alignment with the plans of God in your life. You must confront whatever is blocking you—from your emotions, to your thoughts, to your actions, to your decisions, and your life choices.

When you are united and aligned with God's purpose, you can achieve your desired speed and flow in the right direction—according to God's flight plans. The full force of your emotions, mindset, body, and soul must be focused in one direction—*forward*.

You hear "prepare for take off" every time you get on a plane and prepare to fly from one state to another. Yes, you've bought the ticket. You've committed to the journey. However, there are necessary steps you must take as you "prepare for takeoff."

1.   Prepare for change

It is certain that your destination will be vastly different from your current position. The climate will also be different.

2.   Be patient

It may take some time to get to your destination. You may take a nonstop flight or several flights to get there.

3.   Don't forget to exchange your currency

This journey is about your healing and transformation of your mind, heart, spirit, and body. Don't forget to exchange pain for purpose, unrest for peace, insecurities for self care, hurts for authentic love, fears for faith, residue for redemption, lack of prosperity, doubts for favor, and your past for your freedom!

4. Carry On

Don't quit along the way. When it gets tough, still carry on. One step at a time. Be patient with yourself; you will get there if you keep going in the right direction.

5. .kcab kool t'noD

Don't look back. Your purpose is ahead! The runway is clear, and you are now in position. Look forward; you are about to takeoff!

Quadrant 2
Take Flight

"Have I not commanded you? Be strong and courageous. Do not be terrified; do not be discouraged, for the Lord your God will be with you wherever you go."

—Joshua 1:9

"A mile of a highway will only take you one mile…
But a mile of a runway will take you anywhere!"

—Unknown

So, you've done the work.

You've brought along the important elements that will bring you success and complement your journey.

The check-in process was long, but baggage and chaos are now behind you. You've been waiting for this moment for quite some time.

FROM THE TARMAC TO THE RUNWAY

You're prepared. You packed your bags, and you are officially ready to fly.

As you sit there on the plane, you take a deep breath. You're safe. No more worries about missing your flight or not having a seat. The only thing left for you to do now is wait.

Waiting is a task, so simple, yet at times, it can seem so difficult. When you are ready to move forward, waiting can be unpleasant and trying. Yet, this simple duty that everyone must achieve at some point or another, can make or break your success.

Many people think the arrival or the moment when they take off is more important. However, the time spent on the tarmac is actually more important. Why? Because, it is during this time that the mechanical errors are being rectified. The plane is being refueled and prepared for a successful landing. Without this time of delay, the plane could malfunction at high altitudes, endangering the lives of its passengers.

Isn't it merciful and gracious how God prepares us in a season of delay for the high altitudes we've dreamed about?

Yet, there we sit. Waiting.

W	W	W	W	W
A	A	A	A	A
I	I	I	I	I
T	T	T	T	T
I	I	I	I	I
N	N	N	N	N
G	G	G	G	G

We can be so impatient with life. Certain things require us to be still and wait. And, there are other things in life that require us to move forward, discover our area of improvement, and continue moving forward.

Many times, we move forward in periods designed for us to be still, and we are immobile during times when God has called us forward.

Let's take a further look and examine this theory with airplanes and then, again with life.

If you were on a plane in the air, only to find out the plane has run out of fuel, lives would be at stake. The plane would risk an unsafe landing or a detour without the proper amount of fuel. The passenger's and crew's lives would be at high risk. Time would be lost, and the airline would lose money, credibility, and trust. Additionally, everyone involved would experience an expected amount of frustration.

Now, apply this concept to your life. Picture your situation—your own personal tarmac—the stretch of time spent waiting for your life to take off, elevate, and soar.

As you sit waiting, it may seem that time is passing idly by. However, this is your moment of preparation, refining, strengthening, and equipping for the great journey ahead. The tarmac is the sacred place where you safeguard your future. You are fortifying your mind, body, and soul—you are transforming from the sluggish caterpillar to the nimble butterfly.

Be your best right now where you are so you can be fully ready to experience your best at the next level. Yes, it will be great then, when you get there—but never forget that you are great right now. It is a process. You are learning to trust it. And as you do— get ready for takeoff!

You have made it this far. The runway is clear and ready. It's your time!

N O W

The pilot has spoken with the control tower. The flight plan is set. You are updated on important updates about the weather and your expected arrival time, and the pilot shares their expectations about turbulence, altitude, and the flight plan. The route has been confirmed. You are clear on where you are going and how you will get there.

Ladies and gentlemen, this is your pilot speaking. Welcome aboard. This is a non-stop flight to your purpose. We are getting ready to depart. Please ensure your seat belt is secured, folding trays are upright, and your carry-on is underneath the seat in front of you or in the overhead bin. At this time, all electronic devices need to be set to airplane mode. Flight attendants, please prepare for gate departure. Thank you!

This moment right now is a moment of affirmation and excitement. This is a moment of knowing you are in alignment with your purpose and a deep sense of being on track to experiencing fulfillment. This flight is

		I	I	
		N	M	
		C	P	
S		R	O	
		E	R	!
O		D	T	
		I	A	
		B	N	
		L	T	
		Y		

It is not to be taken for granted. All the time that you've waited on the runway of life is about to pay off.

As you embark on the journey of elevation, you must be cognizant of the rules for elevation. Prepare to shift your way of being, seeing, and living.

The pilot is there to guide your flight, but the control tower oversees the big picture and the master plan so you can safely reach your destination. Well, you also have a flight crew, a team of attendants to ensure your comfort and safety throughout your flight. Be thankful for those God has placed in a position to be apart of your journey.

Just as you leave the concourse, your flight attendant will advise you of the safety procedures. "Put on your own oxygen mask before assisting others."

Before you can help anyone else, you must be in a position of strength and abundance. Otherwise, you and your intention to those you want to help may end up failing. No matter how big your heart is or how much you try, if you want to be good to anyone in any way, first, you must help yourself.

It's contrary to how we think we should operate, but nevertheless, it's an important lesson as you take this flight.

I learned this the hard way. I gave my mask away and eventually found it hard to breathe. I learned to breathe again. With time, I learned to take in air first and secure my own safety. You can't give anyone anything you don't have to give. Let's re-read that together.

YOU

CAN

NOT

GIVE

ANYONE

ANYTHING

YOU

DO

NOT

HAVE

TO

GIVE

You must have air before you can give it to someone else.

This is for those who are too self-sacrificing. This is for the men and women who don't have an identity outside of their family or work. This is for the helpers who don't help themselves. The counselors who deal with everyone else's problems and neglect their own. This is for me and you.

You are no good to help anyone unless you help yourself.

It doesn't matter how big your heart is or how good you try; if you want to serve others in any way, you must refill, revitalize yourself, and ensure your own wellbeing. Then, when it's time for you to give to others, you can give from a place of abundance, prosperity, and strength.

On the other hand, those who struggle with selfishness, pay attention. Once you put on your mask, HELP SOMEONE ELSE! When you are given abundance, prosperity, and strength, share it with others. It's not just about you.

NEXT LEVEL ELEVATION

Elevation is the journey from one position to a higher level. Your perspective, your altitude, your oxygen even changes. As you

```
                        E
                      T
                    A
                  V
                E
              L
            E
```

you begin with an intention, yet you could never be prepared enough for the lessons, revelation, and depth of knowledge and wisdom you will unearth.

Elevation requires deliberate calculation; speed must collide with thrust to produce the power needed to take flight. You must also focus on heading in the right direction.

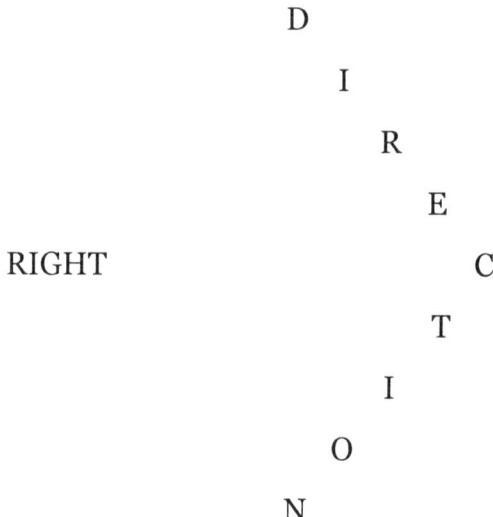

RIGHT DIRECTION

Many flights take off from the same airport, yet destinations can be vast and wide, from north to south, from east to west, across states and even across continents.

Yet once you've committed to God's flight plan for your life, your vision, your goals, your emotions, your thought life, and your actions all should be in harmony.

There are no distractions. The pilot is charged with the responsibility of safely carrying hundreds of passengers across the waters and many lands to a chosen destination.

With all the many possibilities, flights, and flight plans, the pilot cannot focus on someone else's flight plan. He or she must focus their energy, their attention, their aircraft and all forces to move towards the appointed place.

There is a divine flight plan for your life ordained by God. However, it is up to you to focus your mind, heart and soul completely upon the will and plan of God for your life.

Get ready; things are getting ready to accelerate. Every second counts. Focus forward, seize every moment and every opportunity. Are you paying attention?

Now it's time to take off. We can rest now, secure in God's Master Flight Plan and perfect route. Trust and believe - once you take flight, your life will never be the same.

As we taxi into position the bounce of the aircraft comes to a stop on the last turn. All the chaos that's involved with travelling turns to complete stillness at this moment. Hearts race behind calm eyes, and the well-traveled have already fallen asleep. The wheels pause and hold steady the full weight of the aircraft as we face the full length of the runway. The runway confidently calls us onward.

The aircraft proceeds forward, but differently this time, with takeoff thrust. This is your maximum output of power; this is your purpose power!

Your purpose power is used to gain speed quickly so you can transition from one level to the next!

Momentum is necessary during this time. You must know that speed is not the only thing you need to take flight. Your momentum encompasses all of you: mind, body, and spirit. All of who you are must contribute to moving forward quickly at the same time. The word onward gives us a clue as to what to expect, "on war," without ourselves. You will have to fight for all of you, especially your flesh, to be disciplined during this time. It's necessary for the momentum you need.

The more momentum you gain, the more you will notice the wind. In life, wind represents the things that toss us around unexpectedly, but during this time of taking flight, the wind is necessary. The things that happened to us, the hurts that were and may still be present, are now coupled with our purpose and power, which are placed UNDERNEATH us to elevate us upwards and onwards.

Anything in our past that has come against us, coupled with God's grace, will now be used to push our purpose!

These moments on the runway are about your future and your freedom. In each moment, you have to detach from your comfort zone, the things you've held onto, and the things that have held onto you.

The runway is like a capsule of quick and necessary transformations; no one takes flight without them.

As you gain more momentum, you rely less on your support geared for the runway (this world) and more on what you need to take flight in the air (the holy spirit). You know, all the things you thought you needed (accolades, validation from people, a specific persona, luck, trying to fit in with other people, a certain amount of money, approval) yeah, no longer necessary when you are seeking to live your life in purpose.

ALL YOU NEED IS CHRIST JESUS!

Everything you need, He has it for you! You must let go of your dependence on this world and fully trust the Lord.

Just as the wheels on an airplane are only good for the ground, there comes a time when you must spread your wings and fly.

This is our moment of maximum speed. The moment just before the aircraft lifts up, we leave the old behind and enter the new. As you take flight, your speed overcomes the weight of your past, and your vessel operates at full capacity as it is intended to.

```
|          T          |
|          A          |
|          K          |
|          E          |
|                     |
|          F          |
|          L          |
|          I          |
|          G          |
|          H          |
|          T          |
|                     |
| ⅠⅠⅠ  NOW IS YOUR TIME  ⅠⅠⅠ |
```

At this moment, we take flight!

```
                    Y
                    L
            L               F        E
     U              F           H
F                   O       T
─────────────────────────────────────
G       R       O       U       N       D
```

There is an unexplainable feeling of limitlessness as we accelerate upwards.

Rise above. You have heard this call before. I know you have. Remember when you thought you couldn't do it? Well now, you know there are no gaps in God's grace. Rise above. There is still more for you ahead.

Your wings already exist. All you have to do now is fly.

Flight Segment 14
On The Tarmac

It is imperative that as we wait, we are not idle. We do not lose hope or lose patience in this critical time. As we wait for our future to take off – the dream, the marriage, the career, the business, the success we've imagined, the promises God has whispered in our hearts –we prepare ourselves. We are tested, just like that plane. We are examined and prepared for the flight ahead.

This critical time of testing will guarantee our success. As we wait, our future becomes fail-proof. God is building us internally; He is correcting our insecurities and fears.

This is your preparation season. Get ready, hold on to hope, plan for the vision before you, and let patience do its "perfect work". You are becoming more beautiful as you cultivate inner peace, strength, and grace beyond measure.

I was reminded of how my life was on the tarmac one early morning as I flew to Los Angeles. Excited about the trip across the country, I sat on the runway thinking about the time, effort, and planning that would've been required had I driven or taken a train. A plane travels faster with fewer obstacles and stops. I could've traveled by foot or car, taking a similar route, yet the possibilities of reaching my destination quickly, increased greatly, when I decided to take flight.

In the work I did, I developed a degree of notability for working at the state attorney's office. From the outside looking in, others admired my success as though I'd reached my full potential. They saw the size of responsibility, the power, and the impact that was present, yet I understood that I was just getting off the tarmac.

I was destined for a higher elevation.

And, if no one else has told you, YOU ARE TOO!

It was nice to feel accomplished. It felt good to be in a place of comfort and safety. I could have stayed there and been applauded, praised, and reached a certain level of influence that may have satisfied most.

But for those of you who desire the highest level of potential that God has planned for your life, the tarmac is not enough.

But for those of you who desire the highest level of potential that God has planned for your life, the tarmac is not enough.

But for those of you who desire the highest level of potential that God has planned for your life, the tarmac is not enough.

Sure, you've bought the ticket, you've made it beyond security, and you've been seated on the plane. But you've only just begun. You can't stop here. There is another side to this journey, and it looks and feels completely different from yours now.

How many people stay on the tarmac of life? Have you settled on the tarmac?

Your intentions aren't enough. You can purchase a ticket but if you don't show up and get on the plane, it's useless.

There are those who are afraid to fly, so they watch through the windows of the airport in amazement as others bravely take flight. They will never see the destinations, promises, and blessings the other side has to offer.

Where are you on this journey? Have you left home? Are you watching through the windows? Are you comfortable where you are? Where do you want to be?

Not the cry, but the flight of a wild duck leads the flock to fly and follow.

—Chinese proverbs

Flight Segment 15
P&R

The pressure that you feel right now, is simply a means to lift you off the ground. When you know your steps or your flight plans have been ordered by the Lord, you can walk in full confidence. So, even when you stumble, you know you will not fall. But know that every experience has propelled you to the point of taking flight!

Breathe easy

Understand that everything you've done, every prayer, every tear, and every experience up until now, coupled with God's direction, sovereignty, and grace, has equipped you and prepared you to take off.

Pressure is necessary

In addition to the pressure you feel, you will also feel resistance. Right before you level up, it's expected that there is resistance.

Expect Resistance

Resistance occurs when the airplane has to push the air around it; similarly, the faster the airplane is moving, the more resistance it experiences. This resistance is confirmation that you are moving forward with purpose. In aerodynamics, air resistance is called drag. This resistance can show up in the form of doubt, fears, or anything that can

D
R
A
G
YOU
D
O
W
N

if you are not using your purpose power.

Maybe you fear your dream is too big to accomplish?

It's just a little drag. And remember, drag doesn't keep us down; it only reminds us that we are moving forward.

Flight Segment 16
Get off the Roller Coaster

We've all had other thrills in life that we've expected to get us to our destination. We thought some pathways would take us further, but later on

<pre>
D
    O
        W
            N
T
    H
        E
    L
        I
            N
                E,
</pre>

we realized it wasn't a flight we were on. It was a roller coaster ride!

A roller coaster ride represents the emotional highs and lows of life that lead you right back to the same loop where you started. If you continue to travel by means of a roller coaster, it is usually for the amusement of others and/or abuse of self.

This pattern has to stop so you can choose a healthier way to navigate and finally get where you need to go without ending up where you started.

When you fly with God, you are safest.

When you fly with God you move fastest.

When you fly with God, you go further.

Aahhhh. Now settle down; this is not a repeat of your past but a new thing, a purpose thing. You are in the right place, so put your seatbelt on and relax.

It's not about the questions; it's about the source from which you get your answers!

Many people ask questions to those who aren't equipped to answer. We are all guilty of this. There may come times when you feel the urge to ask important questions to just anyone because you need an answer. However, it is your responsibility to protect your most significant questions from the wrong people , as their guidance can mislead your heart and mind. The right answer can be life-changing, but the wrong one can be devastating.

We need to focus on the right source so we can operate on the right information. Information you can trust. If you want to make sure the plane is safe, you need to ask the right person. You wouldn't ask the flight attendant, you would need to ask the avionics engineer for your plane. Make sure you are a getting your confirmation and affirmation from the right person. God will place the right people who are trained and experienced in your life.

N
E
V
E
R
T
H
LESS

The best source is God.

You have permission to go directly to the source for any need. Don't go to anyone other than the source. When God gives you confirmation, there is no need to reconfirm it with your friends, parents, spouse, or whoever else.

Flight Segment 17
<u>V1</u>

Velocity is speed. Did you know God can expedite your speed? Have you been stagnant in your purpose, career, or business for a long time? Well, I have great news for you! When we seek God wholly, He can and will expedite us forward with great speed. No need to hold regret and cry over wasted time. Just repent, turn from the ways that kept you captive, and forward ALL your focus on him.

God can expedite you from the hangar to the runway and from the runway to the sky!

Speed and design are the only two things that can lift an airplane! Speed is your ability to overcome life's weight! As such in life, resilience is your ability to overcome. How resilient are you? Design is your God-given purpose! Who you are at your core. The purest version of who you are.

As we take flight,

HEALING

&

RESILIENCE

&

PURPOSE

are realized.

There are

        NØ limits

                to the magnitude of what God can do in your life and how fast he can turn your situation around!

Flight Segment 18
Lift off to Your Next Level

The runway is the only suitable place to take flight. The runway has been

CREATED

PREPARED & PROTECTED

for this purpose, just as God has

CREATED

PREPARED & PROTECTED

you for His purpose. Because the runway is such a sacred place there are rules to the runway. Lets go deep with the two rules that have the biggest consequences if not followed.

#1 Do not enter the runway without clearance! This is called runway incursion. Runway incursion causes danger to traffic in a protected area.

Our timing and God's timing sometimes do not line up. We want to move forward immediately, not realizing the harm we would place ourselves in as well as others. We must be obedient and listen to the one who is all-knowing. The purpose of the runway will always remain the same, but the difference between our timing and God's timing is the difference between placing yourself on a clear path or directly in harm's way.

#2 Do not overrun the runway! This occurs when you don't lift off before the runway ends, and the aircraft has touched beyond the end of the runway or missed it entirely.

To reduce the possibility of overrunning the runway, you must have a thorough understanding of the interrelationship between having faith and timely obedience.

Overrunning the runway is a direct result of relying more on your support on the ground (this world) than trusting and relying on the Holy Spirit (God).

We can't hold onto the things and comforts of this world and live on purpose at the same time! Misunderstanding the two destabilizes your take off, distorts your runway length, miscalculates the necessary speed you need, and depreciates the risks. Subsequently and consequently neglecting parts of the plane that are geared to assist you.

ONCE GOD HAS GIVEN YOU CLEARANCE ON THE RUNWAY, IT'S YOUR RESPONSIBILITY TO TAKE FLIGHT!

As stated earlier, the runway is a series of transformations. Each of these transformational processes are ones God intends for us to experience so we can not only lift off to our next level but also so we can be empowered to look within and connect with Him in a unique and special way. When we trust in Him, we are empowered to take flight purposefully and have an eagle's eye perspective of all God has in store.

Where would a plane be without a runway?

NO

Similarly, where would we be without grace?

WHERE

Flight Segment 19
<u>Wheels Up</u>

Taking flight would not be possible without wheels and tires. The wheels and tires, that appear so small and insignificant in comparison, hold the full weight of the aircraft. They are designed to withstand extremely heavy loads for short durations.

The tires on an aircraft are filled with pressurized air: the proper pressure level of air gives strength. In addition to strength, the pressure provides durability and the ability to last.

If the pressure in the tires is wrong, it will cause some form of a flat tire or certainty that the tire will explode in due time. If a tire is extremely flat, it will be immobile. Some tires appear full, but they are below the pressurized minimum; these tires do not have the same durability and will malfunction at some point in the future if not addressed. Now, on the flip side, if the tire is overfilled, it will blow up when the airplane is trying to hold its weight and reach its maximum speed.

Is your confidence in your purpose underinflated and your pride in self overinflated?

Did you know that an overinflated tire actually damages the aircraft wheel before the tire? This is the perfect reminder to check your ego because it will harm you and your purpose before it harms anything else!

YOU MUST BE ABLE TO CARRY YOUR PURPOSE WITH HUMILITY.

The small and seemingly insignificant actions, thoughts, and things you do carry weight. Be mindful of everything you do and do it with a humble spirit.

Once in the air, wheels are to be stored away. Also, don't forget that the posture of humility that helped you take flight will always be necessary at every stage of flight. The pilot doesn't disregard the tires once in the air. He keeps them close to the heart of the plane. When the wheels and tires are retracted, they are no longer visible. Similarly, humility does not always have to be visible, but you do need to possess it.

Did you know?

The tires of a Boeing jet landing gear consist of 8 main gear wheels and two nose wheels. This is enough material to make 100 automobile tires.

Flight Segment 20
<u>Dynamics that Simulate Growth</u>

Thrust, drag, weight, and lift are the four forces on an airplane. Although they each maintain different influences on an aircraft, together they enable the aircraft to navigate with purpose. Each opposing dynamic that works against each other is used to create the right equilibrium in order to fly!

Nasa.gov notes that lift works the opposite of weight. Thrust works the opposite of drag. When the forces are balanced, a plane flies in a level direction. The plane goes up if the forces of lift and thrust are more than gravity and drag. If gravity and drag are bigger than lift and thrust, the plane goes down. Just as drag holds something back as a response to the wind flow, lift pushes something up. The air pressure is higher on the bottom side of a wing, so it is pushed upward.

Thrust is the forward force produced by the engine. It opposes or overcomes the force of drag and moves the airplane forward.

What top 3 things motivate you to overcome and move forward?

Drag is a *rearward*, retarding force caused by disruption of airflow by the wing, rotor, fuselage, and other protruding objects. Drag opposes thrust and acts *rearward* parallel to the relative wind. Drag is what slows the aircraft down.

What top 3 things have held you back consistently in your life?

Weight is the combined load of the aircraft, the fuel, the crew, and the cargo/baggage. Weight is a force that pulls the aircraft downward because of the force of gravity.

What top 3 purposes is your life carrying?

Lift is the force that holds an airplane in the air. The wings create most of the lift used by airplanes.

What are the top 3 things or promises from God that lift your spirits no matter the circumstance?

Flight Segment 21
Air Traffic Control

Air traffic control's primary goal is safety. They oversee all the flights in your vicinity to include the unseen aircraft when your vision is impaired or obstructed. Air traffic control maintains control and structure of what is going on in the sky and on the ground. They are in contact with all aircraft, incoming and outgoing and they systematically organize all flights within proper timing. The air traffic control team is always paying attention because they are responsible for thousands of lives every second of the day! Additionally, air traffic control understands and communicates the proper altitudes needed to navigate the storms and winds.

Air traffic control is symbolic of a whole language of inner intuition. Inner intuition is the ability of hearing God's voice and understand His signals geared to get us to our destination.

You must listen to the directives given to help you. Pilots know that they cannot see everything, and they know they need help, do you? Pilots also know that lives are depending on them to listen and be obedient in order for them to survive, do you?

Flight Segment 22
Bird Strikes

Airplanes are not the only things with wings roaming the clear blue skies. Birds are often taking flight of their own when they collide with an airplane, which is called a bird strike. Although this does not occur frequently, birds can get caught in a plane's engine during or shortly after take off and destroy the engine of an airplane. Bird strikes pose a high risk and may have deadly results, but they are rarely talked about.

What in your life is a "small thing" but can be devastating to your future?

Lying

Cutting corners

Numbing yourself with alcohol

Procrastinating

These "small things" may not be causing you much of an issue now, but at the next level, they may be deadly in your pursuit of purpose.

Flight Segment 23
Airplane Mode

Airplane mode is rarely used in today's society other than in flight. It is the disabling of connections and staying completely focused on God and where he is taking you. It is so necessary to disconnect from your norm in order to engage in flight mode. Contrary to what most believe, your cellular device doesn't interfere with the plane's electronic systems. The reason airplane mode is required is simply to engage your full attention! When we declutter all other voices, texts, and communication services that are irrelevant, we gain clarity.

God has something really important to tell you, and He needs your FULL ATTENTION!

In airplane mode, the voice that should have always been the loudest is the only voice you now hear.

Flight Segment 24
<u>Altitude</u>

As the airplane continues to rise, your perspective changes dramatically. The view you had below was so

small

and the view you

have now is so

vast.

Your altitude changes your perspective.

God requires us to change our perspective!

God has new heights for us!

God is waiting on us to get in his word, to live out our purpose, and to choose healing and live in freedom!

I believe it is our attitude that determines our altitude. It is the attitude that allows us to soar above those things that would otherwise overcome us.

—T.D Jakes

The higher we soar, the smaller we appear to those who cannot fly."

—Anon

Flight Segment 25
__Cloud 9__

Cloud 9 is an expression that describes a state of pure bliss and joy. I've heard people say I was on cloud 9 after I got married, and then I quickly fell off after a month. Many people think this is a place but it is actually a state of being. Cloud 9 is where many people get stuck and, in relationships, where people fall from the most. I don't want you to be stuck here, so let's get your head out of the clouds. Most think Cloud 9 is a destination they visit, not understanding that it is a place within themselves where they create joy regardless of their circumstance and a place within that can be shared with others.

Flight Segment 26
<u>GO</u>

It is possible to go somewhere you cannot get to in your own power. From this day forward, know that your purpose in God is the only vessel to take you where you truly desire to go! God can and will take you places. Your purpose is the plane that will take you to all the places you could have never gone without it.

For once you have tasted flight, you will walk the earth with your eyes turned skywards, for there you have been, and there you will long to return.

—*Leonardo da Vinci*

Quadrant 3
Soar

"Humble yourselves, then, under God's mighty hand, so that he will lift you up in his own good time. Leave all your worries with him, because he cares for you."

—1 Peter 5:6-7

According to flight experts, there are nearly 10,000 airplanes in the sky at any given moment!

Rise

above

it

ALL,

it's

time

to

SOAR!

There will be elements that you have to navigate as you take flight and begin to soar. It could be rain, storms, heavy winds, lightining, along with other frightful distractions. Some of these you will have the opportunity to avoid, and some you must face head on. For the storms you must face head on, DO NOT FEAR.

"Do not fear, for I am with you; do not be dismayed, for I am your God. I will strengthen you and help you; I will uphold you with my righteous right hand."

—Isaiah 41:10

Though it can be scary, uncomfortable, and rough, you must:

Pay close attention to the fact that God knows you will be confronted with fear and he tells you in advance exactly what to do. God tells us to KNOW that He is with us. I know some of my darkest moments in life were times I felt alone and times I was physically alone. But our God is ALWAYS with us!

God also tells us that he will use the fear you are facing to strengthen you! So the thing you fear is the same thing God uses to strengthen you! Now, that's God! God is a God of faith, strength, and peace; the devil is a god of fear, unrest, and hopelessness.

Fear is the devil's weapon of choice!

If the devil can create fear in your mind or heart, he can begin to control the things you do and, ultimately where you go by controlling where you don't go.

But not you, and not us. We are called to BREAK THROUGH the storm and see the sunshine!

A completely different perspective and a stronger you, awaits you after you rise above the storms.

"When something bad happens, you have three choices. You can let it define you, let it destroy you, or let it strengthen you."

—Theodor Seuss Geisel

Dr. Seuss

Congratulations. You are airborne. You sit in a state of peace and tranquility and the momentum has started to build. As you leave the past behind and as you settle into this new state – you sigh, breathing deeply, taking in the magnificence of the white, rolling heavens before you. All of a sudden, you feel a rumbling. At first, you brush it off, hoping it will pass. But the rumbling builds to a thunder. Your anxiety thickens to fear. Doubts begin to arise.

You are experiencing turbulence.

These pockets of stress, anxiety, and doubt are almost certain. Similar to every phase of life, there will be growing pains, setbacks, unexpected failures, and heartaches. Know that they are only for a moment. This, too shall pass. If you hang on, show patience, and never give up—you will get to your destination. Continue the course. Turbulence is only a minor part of the journey.

During flight, the one thing that most people are startled by the most is turbulence.

TURBULENCE

Flight experts describe turbulence as interference in the air/airflow, which causes an aircraft to move up and down, side to side, or in an unpredictable manner. Turbulence symbolizes unpredictable changes in our lives that range from minor to chaotic.

During the creation of this book, I was blessed enough to connect with Dr. Michael Tatonetti, who is a man of God, a husband, father, speaker, educator, and the author of "Do Meaningful Work." He shared with me his in-flight experience with extreme turbulence. I know his testimony will profoundly impact you as it did me.

Dr. Michael Tatonetti shared that he was in Europe for a conference and was travelling to Barcelona. One thing you must know is that Dr. Michael Tatonetti loves to fly and travel. Air travel was not new to him, but it was always just as exciting. He is the type of man you see in first class reading a book the entire flight, calm, composed, and cool as if sitting in the local bookstore. Dr. Michael Tatonetti described flying as empowering as he takes time to embrace feelings of gratitude as he experiences God's creation from the skies above. "I have never been shaken up by flying; fear did not exist around flying," were his words. For him travel was a form of worship for God.

On his journey home, his flight was delayed due to weather conditions. No flights could take off or land, so he was rerouted to the next flight with a stop in a different country than he initially planned.

Halfway into Dr. Michael Tatonetti's 90-minute flight, the plane started to experience turbulence. He was cool though; remember, he was used to turbulence so his tolerance for turbulence was high. He was experiencing the usual level of turbulence, the level his faith was comfortable with. The kind of turbulence that occurs when the flight attendants are still up walking and those in charge are still smiling.

What he was not used to is what happened next. The turbulence did not clear for a long period of time and became more and more violent. The plane started shifting sideways and the wings of the aircraft started to bend. Passengers began vomiting, screaming, and crying.

THIS WAS A CRISIS!

He was without the knowledge that wings were meant to bend, so it terrified him. On top of also being without the knowledge he would make it safely to the ground.

THIS WAS HIS REALITY IN THE MOMENT BUT NOT THE FINAL OUTCOME!

Similar to Dr. Michael Tatonetti's experience, in life, there is a certain level of adversity that we can manage and tolerate on our own. Once adversity increases, past our comfort zone, and pass the grip of our control, our faith is truly challenged.

During our discussion, Dr. Michael Tatonetti related his experience of being tossed in the skies to the experience of the disciples being tossed in a sea storm with Jesus. The issues were the same: wind. Dr. Michael Tatonetti explained that prior to his experience, he could not quite understand why the disciples did not trust Jesus after all He had already done for them. He couldn't grasp how they allowed fear to overcome them when they were with the one who worked miracles. After his experience, Dr. Michael Tatonetti empathized greatly with the disciples. He realized that although the storm was beyond his control, he has direct access to the one who controls it.

YOU HAVE DIRECT ACCESS TO THE CREATOR OF THE UNIVERSE!

Dr. Michael Tatonetti, recentered his focus on the one who is able in the most unstable of times. He realized that if God permits anything to occur or not occur, then it is in accordance with His will.

Lord, let your will be done.

Dr. Michael Tatonetti's airplane eventually landed safely. Although that experience was traumatic, he eventually returned to the skies and continued his worship and his purpose work across the globe. He credits his recovery to God's sovereignty.

There is not one piece of cosmic dust that is outside the scope of God's sovereign providence.

—*R.C. Sproul*

God is sovereign even over the unstructured and chaotic aspects of our lives. Even when things seem to be flying apart in chaos, God is still in control.
—Unknown Author

Romans 12:2

Do not be conformed to this world, but be transformed by the renewal of your mind, that by testing you may discern what is the will of God, what is good and acceptable and perfect.

(English Standard Version)

Sensitivity to God

There are a myriad of high-end technology sensor systems on airplanes geared to make air travel safe. Sensors give the pilot and the air traffic controller valuable feedback about the condition of the plane and the forecast for the flight. Every system and every sensor supports the pilot, helps navigate the plane, and controls the flight.

If you compare the sensors to other seemingly more important parts, like the engine, the sensors can seem so insignificant, especially in comparison to the size of an airplane.

Faulty sensors can cause a breakdown immediately. As such, in life, we have to pay attention to our sensors. Yes, those small, seemingly insignificant prompts that come up to guide us and serve as warnings.

God is in the details!

In recent events, during the writing of this book, there have been back-to-back fatal plane crashes, in what the early investigation has determined to be the result of faulty sensors.

Two faulty sensors are believed to have caused two planes to go down, killing hundreds in minutes. In our lives, we can have purpose and passion, and have it all right in front of us. But, faulty sensors can completely redirect or even destroy our ability to arrive successfully at our destination. If our sensors are faulty and we are operating based on emotion, that can threaten our future and even annihilate the person God has called us to be! Faulty sensors have the capability to obliterate destiny in moments. If you allow one suicidal thought to take root, it can completely take you down in a moment. One thought can penetrate your being if you are not cognizant of your own faulty sensors and you accept that negative thought.

Yes, there are important goals to be met, relationships to be developed, and opportunities to be had; however, the sensors of your mind and emotions can affect every element of your purpose.

Remain sensitive to the changing dynamics of your flight and how your sensors are responding. Whose voice is echoing/traveling throughout your mind? There may be people that tell you that you aren't worth it or that you won't make it. You have disconnected from those people, but did you disconnect from what they spoke over you?

Everyone has their own perception, and sometimes they will impose those perceptions on you. When others impose their perceptions on you, there can be positive and negative impacts. So be sure to filter in the right influences that will enhance your journey and not drain or distract you from your purpose.

Check your sensors, make sure they are not faulty and working properly.

Once your sensors are working for your good, its time to SOAR in autopilot.

At a certain point in the flight, the plane can ride on autopilot. All the settings, altitude, speed, and direction have been predetermined. The pilot can relax and monitor to ensure the flight plan is going as planned.

What are your autopilot settings? There are some people with positive settings; they are determined to go higher, think positively, show kindness, persist through challenges, and reach their goals.

However, there are other people who have been programmed with negative autopilot settings. They struggle with thoughts of depression, fear, paranoia, insecurities, anxiety, and doubt.

Evaluate your current autopilot settings. These are the cycles that you carry out in your thoughts, words, actions, and behaviors. What belief systems do you carry with you wherever you go?

The autopilot setting will influence your destination. If the settings are correct, then you will be happy with the outcomes. It's good to be in a place where your autopilot settings match your goals. You are committed and in alignment with your vision and God's best for your life.

Your daily habits, lifestyle, behaviors, words, eating practices, energy, and intentions should be aligned with your destination.

Yet, there are times when we revert to a negative autopilot. Our systems and beliefs have become very destructive. Our habits and ways of doing things can be so askew that it can be difficult to regain control. In these cases, there must be a manual override of the flight.

The autopilot setting, contrary to our goals and contrary to our growth, needs to be changed drastically and immediately. This is the place where many crash. The autopilot settings weren't right to begin with. It can seem impossible to get back on track if you don't regain control here.

It's time to pray, ask God, and reconnect with the air traffic controller of your life so he may redirect you back to the master flight plan He has mapped out for your life.

It's time to hit the auto-reset button!

This manual override requires careful listening and intentional progress.

I want to challenge you to think about areas of your life where you need to regain control. You have been drifting in autopilot, allowing anger, fear, anxiety, insecurity, passivity, procrastination, and other negative cycles to take over your life.

Time is steadily slipping by. You have to make a decision to move your life back in the direction that you desire.

You can do it; do it now!

There is nothing safer than flying. Flying isn't dangerous; crashing is what's dangerous.

—*Unknown Author*

Interesting Statistic:

There is a 1 in approximately 12 million chance of dying in an airplane crash versus a 1 in approximately 5 thousand chance of dying in an automobile crash.

Failure saves lives. In the airline industry, every time a plane crashes, the probability of the next crash is lowered by that. Although people died, failure was not in vain.

—*Nassim Nicholas Taleb*

The most unspoken aspect of flying during flight is the crashing part. But like everything else in life, in business, and in relationships, failure is a possibility.

The top reasons planes crash are lack of fuel, pilot fatigue, pilot mishandling, and mechanical issues. These are all metaphors of our internal structures. Many flight experts attribute crashes to a combination of direct and indirect factors, not just one single issue.

This is important to digest now so that you can avoid these issues ahead.

Lack of Fuel to Fuel for the journey

The word of God is the only thing that can sustain you!

The fruits of the spirit are your fuel.

Make sure your physical body is cared for and can finish the race it's intended to run. Feed your body what it needs for your journey.

Pilot Fatigue to Resilient Clarity & Mental Alertness

Fatigue is a result of lack of rest. We must take time to rest.

Fatigue is also a result of trying to do it all on your own until you become completely disoriented. No one wants to live their life going nowhere but in circles. God wants us to call on Him for guidance in every aspect of our lives, great and small. Ask God to give you wisdom and direct you full speed ahead to your purpose.

We must see everything through grace; that is how we find peace, resilience, and clarity.

Pilot Mishandling to Maintaining Your Power

Attention to detail is critical to actualizing the big picture.

You will not be able to do everything, but do what you can every day to maximize your potential and your purpose power. Success comes with consistency.

There is power in your voice. Use it, don't misuse it! Don't let anyone muzzle your voice and your testimony.

Mechanical Issues to Mechanically Working for My Good

Everything is working together for your good. Each engine light you thought was a delay on the ground has been your saving grace in the sky, and each light that comes on will alert you to give attention to the issues developing that you did not know existed.

Religion is mechanical; the relationship with God is real! Watch God move in your life! He is always moving, but are you paying attention?

Be strict when it comes to yourself and soul care. Life wears on us; no one is exempt. Take time to be still. Checking on others is good, but don't forget to check on yourself. Check and change your filters (the mechanism that blocks impurities inward) and parts (the way you go about things/your system of being) timely. Just as an airplane requires ongoing care so do you!

You probably thought this quadrant of the book was where you sit back, relax, and enjoy the flight. I thought so too, until the Holy Spirit guided my words. I've come to learn that soaring is actually where you are most disciplined, where most are required of you, and where you have to be most resilient with everything that you go through!

Soar in grace when you are tempted to quit. Soar in grace when fear comes to shake you. Soar in grace when chaos comes to distract you. Soar in grace when you are tempted to wallow in grief. Soar in grace and make your requests known to God.

Soar in grace during a change of plans.

Soar in grace as you speak the truth.

Soar in grace, and do not be anxious.

Soar in grace and give glory to God.

Soar in grace, prayer, and thanksgiving.

Soaring in Grace is where our testimonies reside.

Soar through the valleys where darkness is only the absence of light.

In my life, things have happened to me that left me feeling purposeless and incredibly vulnerable. Those experiences left me believing that a crash landing was inevitable. I wasn't sure where life was taking me, and I wasn't sure if I even wanted to find out. I remember the call of God by means of a vision of my future. That vision gave me the confidence to know that I would make it if I trusted God over my current circumstances. I began to see the big picture without seeing anything at all in front of me. I began shifting in a new direction even though my flight was far from the perfect path I thought I should have been on. I began making decisions from a place of clarity and hope instead of destruction. The inevitable was no longer inevitable. I just had to tap into the grace that was always there for me and the grace that is always there for you.

Soar through the valleys where there was once darkness until you became the light.

One can never change the past, only the hold it has on you, and while nothing in your life is reversible, you can reverse it nevertheless.

—Merle Shain

"May the God of hope fill you with all joy and peace as you trust in him, so that you may overflow with hope by the power of the Holy Spirit."

—Romans 15:13

Trust God in every situation in your life!

Flight Segment 27
Air Pressure Changes

When you take flight, your environment changes and impacts you. Your physical body also responds to those changes. In most cases, healthy passengers tolerate the air pressure well. The same pressure that elevates you also reduces your oxygen level to a certain degree. If the oxygen level is minimized greatly, then adjustments need to be made. When the oxygen levels drop significantly, oxygen masks, which are a true symbol of additional spiritual self-care, are released from overhead. Isn't God so gracious to release lifelines when we need them? Even more, God is so gracious to have pre-placed them ahead of our journey!

Atmospheric pressure is a force in our lives. For some, there is more pressure in your career, pressure from family, pressure in the area of your finances, pressure from your social circles, or pressure from yourself. The force and its impact are more noticeable the higher you elevate.

> Pressure
> Determines
> Performance.

Is the pressure you are experiencing elevating you or stifling you?

Are your closest friends elevating you or stifling you?

Is your money mindset elevating you or stifling you?

Is your integrity elevating you or stifling you?

Are your eating habits elevating you or stifling you?

Are your beliefs elevating you or stifling you?

The beautiful thing about air pressure changes is the fact that you can make changes. You can make changes so the changes work in your favor!

Did you know?

Oxygen masks provide less than 15 minutes' worth of oxygen because that is more than a sufficient amount of time for a pilot to descend to a breathable altitude.

Flight Segment 28
<u>Storms of Life</u>

As we take flight, any distractions can be catastrophic. The distractions of doubt, fear, procrastination, and old stale stories left unchecked have the potential to slow down, stagnate, and completely stop us from getting to our destination.

However, if we push through, we will see the sunshine ahead in that higher place.

What storms have tried to delay your promise? What threshold have you had to break in order to see the sunshine?

When you go higher and refocus on the elevated place, you can make it to that place beyond your struggle to a place of beauty and clarity.

As we go higher, God allows us to not only walk in the light of Christ, but we gain the capacity to shine our light for those who will come after us. See the beauty in your journey. See yourself and your story the way God sees you. God wants to use your life to bring Him glory.

Flight Segment 29
Thrive Through Turbulence

Turbulence is to an airplane as uncertainty is to life. It's usually unexpected, and it is bound to happen. Because we know this, we must also know how to thrive through turbulence.

Turbulence has differing degrees of intensity. Let's use light, moderate, and vigorous as an illustration.

Each degree can only truly be determined by the perception of the person experiencing it. Their experiences, resilience and their faith will be factors in how they process the turbulence in their life.

Light turbulence represents a minimal disruption to your life, minimal challenge to your faith, and minimal use of your resiliency reserve. Many people have overcome the light turbulence life has brought. This level of turbulence is expected, so most prepare for it in advance.

Moderate turbulence represents an uncomfortable and more intense feeling that circumstances are out of control. There are simultaneously competing forces for faith and worry. Some have never experienced moderate turbulence in life, but most certainly, those reading this book have experienced it, or you may even be experiencing it now. This is the level of turbulence is very uncomfortable and it will either build up a level of tolerance or force you to surrender to fear.

Vigorous turbulence is a level of turbulence that most wish not to ever encounter. It is the deeply disturbing experiences and traumas of life. It's the experiences that can leave most internally wounded and shaken.

As turbulence is well within what an aircraft is designed to fly through, you are well within the grace designed to work all things together for your good.

Every degree of turbulence can be overcome by grace!

Your most profound and intimate experiences of worship will likely be in your darkest days-when your heart is broken, when you feel abandoned, when you're out of options, when the pain is great and you turn to God alone.

—Rick Warren

Life has taught me
I am not always in control. Life is full of experiences, lessons, heartbreak, and pain. But it has also shown me love, beauty, possibility, and new beginnings. Embrace it all. It makes us who we are, and after every storm comes a clear sky.
—Unknown Author

Flight Segment 30
Just Wing It

In everything you do, your focus must remain forward. Your journey will not be at the same altitude throughout the entire flight and we know it will not be a straight path to your destination, much less a smooth one. We now find confidence knowing that our "**heart in stomach feeling**" only means **we have reached a**

HIGHER

```
                              L
                         E
                   V
              E
         L                    ↑
```

Whether we feel fully prepared or not, now is the time to wing it!

Wings make it possible for an airplane to fly!

Your wings are your purpose, your passions, and the things that matter to the heart of God.

Do those things relentlessly, unapologetically, and consistently. Perfectly or imperfectly.

Don't allow over-thinking, perfectionism, resistance, and doubt to steal your momentum.

Your wings already exist,
All you have to do now is SOAR!

You are destined for greatness!

Believe in yourself

&

Go for it!

ONE DAY   OR   ANYONE
DEAD   DAY

(letters arranged vertically)

O   D
N D   OR   A O
E A   Y N
   Y   E

YOU DECIDE!

Flight Segment 31
On the Fly

We are soaring thousands of miles above the skyscrapers and towers that used to tower over us. The speed that initially pushed us deeper into our seats is now weightless as we move five hundred-plus miles per hour, even though it may feel like we are not moving at all. The immutable, overbearing mass of the plane that once felt heavy and stagnant is now boundless and light on the backdrop of an endless sky. Enjoy the expanded feeling of freedom the moment has to offer. And, even though you are on the fly, don't forget to enjoy each moment of the journey.

Flight Segment 32
Tailwind

Wind can propel you forward, take you off track, or slow you down!

Headwind

Headwind blows against the direction you are going. Headwind slows you down, reduces your speed, and decreases your performance while using more fuel.

Tailwind

Tailwind blows in the same direction of travel as you. Tailwind is favorable as it increases performance, reduces fuel usage, and gives you more momentum.

Crosswind

Crosswind blows perpendicular to you. Crosswind makes flying more difficult and dangerous. Crosswinds are unpredictable.

Winds makes the pilot maneuver. Soaring is not passive; soaring is active! You must strategically know how to deal with wind so it pushes you forward.

But

Doesn't

To soar, you must also be coordinated.

You have to be skilled at making all you efforts work together. Your spiritual health should be working alongside your mental health. Your physical health should be working alongside your emotional health. Your actions should be working alongside your goals.

&

When you come across that blinking red sensor, you have to maneuver quickly; your ability to coordinate and strategize reduces the negative impact of wind!

What we need to do is always lean into the future; when the world changes around you and when it changes against you-what used to be a tailwind is now a headwind- you have to lean into that and figure out what to do because complaining isn't a strategy.

—Jeff Bezos

Flight Segment 33
<u>Hijacked</u>

The enemy desires to hijack your dreams, your vision, and your purpose. Notice I deliberately used the word "your!" The enemy isn't after just random dreams, visions, and purpose; the enemy is after what belongs to you!! If you own it, the enemy wants to seize and hijack it! Most hijackers claim to have explosives and don't have the power or means of threat they claim they do. Remember, the enemy's weapon of choice is fear, and remember, the enemy comes to steal, kill, and destroy!

What has held your dreams hostage?

What negotiations have taken place with your hijackers?

What has demanded your flight to be diverted?

We no longer negotiate when it comes to our purpose, our dreams, our health, our mental health, our peace, and our instructions from God! We must disarm the hijackers with our faith, our obedience, and our prayers! The enemy's plot against you will be foiled.

Anything or anyone who has tried to hijack your purpose now has to surrender to authorities (God).

Pslam 91 (KJV)

He that dwelleth in the secret place of the most High shall abide under the shadow of the Almighty. I will say of the LORD, He is my refuge and my fortress: my God; in him will I trust. Surely he shall deliver thee from the snare of the fowler, and from the noisome pestilence. He shall cover thee with his feathers, and under his wings shalt thou trust: his truth shall be thy shield and buckler. Thou shalt not be afraid for the terror by night; nor for the arrow that flieth by day; nor for the pestilence that walketh in darkness; nor for the destruction that wasteth at noonday. A thousand shall fall at thy side, and ten thousand at thy right hand; but it shall not come nigh thee. Only with thine eyes shalt thou behold and see the reward of the wicked. Because thou hast made the LORD, which is my refuge, even the most High, thy habitation; there shall no evil befall thee, neither shall any plague come nigh thy dwelling. For he shall give his angels charge over thee, to keep thee in all thy ways. They shall bear thee up in their hands, lest thou dash thy foot against a stone. Thou shalt tread upon the lion and adder: the young lion and the dragon shalt thou trample under feet. Because he hath set his love upon me, therefore will I deliver him: I will set him on high, because he hath known my name. He shall call upon me, and I will answer him: I will be with him in trouble; I will deliver him, and honour him. With long life will I satisfy him, and shew him my salvation.

Flight Segment 34
Layovers

    Layovers are not the final stops. They are just temporary pauses on the journey. Sometimes the gap in travel can take longer than the actual flight remaining to get where you need to go. On several occasions, I've seen people sprawled out in the airport, dreadfully waiting for their connecting flight, waiting to reach their destination. Some even fall asleep and miss their flight! On the other hand, I've also seen some racing to their connecting flight with only minutes to make it across the terminal.

    Have you experienced a layover on your journey onward? I know I have experienced a few. Unplanned layovers can be unexpected grief, illness, or trauma. There are also layovers you create with your decisions. Lack of selfcare, disobedience, sin, ill-preparedness, and poor stewardship of your time are unnecessary layovers that we created.

~A Stop En route~

    Isn't it just like God to reminds us that our stop en route isn't a stop in grace! You may feel like you are starting all over but you are not! You are still on your way!

    Whether your layover is short or long, don't get comfortable or complacent during your layover! Always be ready for the next segment of your journey.

EVENTUALLYEVERTHINGCONNECTS

Flight Segment 35
Fear Factor

We know for sure that fear is one of the enemy's weapons against us living out our purpose, and we know that we must choose our autopilot of faith over fear! We know that fear comes as a precursor to our next level. Fear will always present itself before your next level. We also know not to allow fear, worry, and anxiety to overwhelm us or cement us in the past or present.

Many are consumed in fear by political unrest, racial violence, natural disasters, infectious viruses, war, terrorism, fluctuating economic climate, and an unable financial future that they live in fear every single day.

There is fear all around us,

B

U

T

We don't have to live in fear!

Fear is designed to stop you and control you. How many times has fear robbed you from taking flight towards your goals and dreams and from being courageous?

The biggest factor that can prevent you from getting to your destination is fear! You ever notice how even after there has been a plane crash, most people still decide to travel? They are still doing what they need to do in order to get where they need to go. Never let fear stop you from getting where God wants you to go. Someone else's experiences and fears do not have to be yours. You are prepared, you are built, and you are cut out for this. Stop letting fear stop you!

Feeling fear and operating in fear are two different things. Operate in faith even if you feel afraid! Go ahead, do it afraid!

"We must choose to override our fears to pursue our passions."

—Jeff Spires

Override means to cancel the automatic response and use your power to supersede it. In life, there are times when we have to set a manual override! The times when we need a huge shift and the times we need to get clear, we must override our normal tendencies. When you start to see your good habits fading and your old habits returning, you can override them with faith and discipline.

I thought in depth about what keeps people flying after incidents and what overrides they need to use to mentally, emotionally, and spiritually proceed despite of fear. I landed here.

Resilience

Guts

Drive

Determination

Will

Faith

Relentlessness

Hope

Grit

Confidence in your calling

Grace

Forward thinking

Making your purpose non-negotiable

Knowing who is on your side (God).

"Fear not, for I am with you; Be not dismayed, for I am your God. I will strengthen you, Yes, I will help you, I will uphold you with My righteous right hand. …I will strengthen you, Yes, I will help you, I will uphold you with My righteous right hand."

—Isaiah 41:10

Flight Segment 36
<u>Pardon Me</u>

Things happen. From tarmac to tarmac we bump into people, walk into things, and we move on. The journey isn't perfect, and neither are we. A pardon is a forgiveness, complete freedom from wrongdoing. There will be times you need to be pardoned, and times you need to extend a pardon.

Pardon me, it seems to be the easiest out of the two. So, let's focus on extending a pardon. We are called by God to extend a pardon to those who do us wrong. We cannot ask God to pilot our plane but refuse to give him access to the cockpit of our hearts.

Do you want God or unforgiveness piloting your aircraft?

"Forgive others, not because they deserve forgiveness, but because you deserve peace."

—*Jonathan Lockwood Huie*

Flight Segment 37
Precious Cargo Onboard

You are valuable,

You have been regarded with extreme importance to God,

You are esteemed,

Crafted with extraordinary consideration,

You are God's masterpiece,

Carefully created to His liking,

You are significant!

Your needs, your safety, and your protection are God's priority.

God loves you so much!

You are the apple of His eye,

But sometimes we see ourselves differently;

We forgot our value and become reckless,

Forgetting our worth but worthy just the same,

So,

God wants to remind you,

On this journey of life, You are precious cargo!

Can anything ever separate us from Christ's love? Does it mean He no longer loves us if we have trouble or calamity, or are persecuted, or hungry, or destitute, or in danger, or threatened with death? …No, despite all these things, overwhelming victory is ours through Christ, who loved us. And I am convinced that nothing can ever separate us from God's love. Neither death nor life, neither angels nor demons, neither our fears for today nor our worries about tomorrow — not even the powers of hell can separate us from God's love. No power in the sky above or in the earth below — indeed, nothing in all creation will ever be able to separate us from the love of God that is revealed in Christ Jesus our Lord.

—Romans 8:35, 37-39

Flight Segment 38
<u>Flying First Class</u>

First class is a way of life, not just a seating arrangement on a flight! Luxury is a wealth of healing. Luxury is enjoying a present moment in time. Luxury is opulent wellbeing. Luxury is quality of life. Luxury is prosperous health. Luxury is financial abundance. Luxury is a limitless mindset.

Luxury is Freedom!

Luxury lives in the finer details of your decisions. Give yourself permission to live better; your first-class life is attainable! You have the freedom to decide. Your possibilities are endless. Make your life full by fully using your God-given gifts and talents. Dream big and live even bigger. Set your standard higher and own God's best for your life. Value your freedom! Live out your calling!

~~No more excuses~~

~~No more regret~~

~~No more willingness to settle~~

~~No more low self-worth~~

~~No more low standards~~

~~No more laziness~~

~~No more hiding~~

~~No more following the herd~~

~~No more poor morale character~~

~~No more lack of self integrity~~

~~&~~

~~No more B$~~

A LIFE OF FREEDOM IS THE BEST WAY TO USE THE GRACE WE ARE GIVEN!

Flight Segment 39
N.E.S.W

Nevertheless, Everyday, Shift & Soar, With God

Nevertheless, is one of the most powerful words you can use to transform your life!

(Insert all your insecurities here)

NEVERTHELESS,

God can and will use you right now!

Every day is a gift. Every day, wake up with thanksgiving in your heart. Pray every day! Make every moment count. Don't take a single day for granted. Every day, God can use you where you are.

Shift and soar. Shift as needed. Truth is necessary, and change is good. Be bold and determined; no need to second guess what the Holy Spirit placed on your heart. Go forth and do great things.

With God all things are possible. Don't try and go it alone in your own strength. You were made for dependence and reliance upon Him. With God, you cannot fail.

"The purpose of life is a life of purpose."

—Robert Byrne

QUAD 4

Landing On Purpose

"For I know the plans I have for you," declares the LORD, "plans to prosper you and not to harm you, plans to give you hope and a future."

—Jeremiah 29:11

Godspeed

The vision, the calling and the purpose full speed ahead!

As the plane begins to descend from the skies, you realize what was prior is nothing in comparison to what is ahead! We are full speed ahead to our destiny. Even if you wanted to go back you don't have enough fuel.

The past is behind you now! Thousands of miles far gone, you have done the brave thing. Distance has extended its grace on your journey onward, and you finally feel close to your destiny. It is a feeling of becoming; you are no longer where you used to be and not yet where you intend to be.

You do, however, have everything you need to land on purpose. All your focus must remain on your purpose now. Getting the aircraft safely on the ground is crucial; there is no time for carelessness and certainly no time for panic at this stage.

For landing, you must do three things: follow instructions, communicate with air traffic control, and wait for clearance to land.

<u>Without God, guiding you, this is impossible.</u>

Don't think you can take it from here on your own! Many want to trust God until they feel they can do it on their own. Don't be mistaken, you need God.

```
                        WAY
                  THE
             OF
        STEP
EVERY
             SECOND
                  HOUR
                        DAY!
```

He is the one who is greater than every

```
H
I         & every      L
G                          O
H                              W!
```

Don't get so caught up in getting where you are going that you forget to rely upon God. Independence is an indicator that you have become your own god, and that is the quickest way to crash. In a world that praises independence, stay deeply dependent on God. You weren't meant to do this alone! It's impossible for you to be the air traffic controller and the pilot and the crew and the passenger and the safety team and the engineer at the same time. Plus, you don't have to. Sometimes God calls us to be one thing, but we are distracted trying to be twenty things. This again, will only result in our demise, burning up fuel going in several directions needlessly.

This only causes burnout, the early downfall of the altitudes we need to maintain to safely reach our destination.

On the other wing of this, Don't get so busy with your purpose that you forget the One who graced your purpose! We need God as we land on purpose, just as we needed God when we were in turbulent times.

Follow instructions

You need to tune in and tune out at the same time. The radio transmission will be filled with chatter, and most of you won't understand, but what is most important is that you know the voice of God, so when He speaks, you recognize it. An untrained ear lacks discernment and to get good at discerning the voice of the Lord, you need practice. God's voice will ignite your entire being and command more from you; that's how you know it is Him. God should be the only guiding factor in our life, not our finances, not our memories, not our family expectations, not our jobs, or our wants. Following God's instructions, at times, will go against all of the above; it will challenge your faith as it is meant to. Listening to and obeying divine direction is necessary.

Communicate

Communication is a two-way street. Are you making time for God? All the airplane technology in the world still cannot replace your need for direct communication. God not only wants to hear from you in time of need, but also in every time. The more time we spend with God, the closer we will be to Him. The more time we spend with God, the closer we will be to our destiny. The more time we spend with God, the closer we get to fulfillment. Praise Him and acknowledge Him in all you do. Just like air traffic control is standing by, God is always there, ready to engage. There is nothing too small or insignificant to call on Him for.

Two things air traffic control will ask a pilot are their distance and their fuel, which will determine the specifications and priority for landing. In order to know how far away you are, you have to know exactly where you are currently. And, in order to ensure you will make it, you have to know how much fuel you have remaining to make it to your destination. This is reflective of our goals and energy output. Do our short-term goals lend themselves to our purpose? Are we expending energy towards our day jobs, just going in circles, and not towards our purpose? Are we short on fuel and long on distance?

Cleared for landing

The pilot confirmed calculations in preparation for arrival. You are now cleared for landing. You have permission. You have the green light. You have full access. You have authorization. Now, it's up to you to reach your full potential. Own it, it's yours, and it's in you! All you have to do now is finish strong!

The descent continues as the airplane levels downward in stages, adjusting to the expected destination. Each movement is modified and deliberate. Although the speed of the aircraft slows, this is the time to accelerate your purpose.

This is the time you dreamt of. This is the reward for your resilience. Your purpose will change this world. Your purpose is needed for such a time as this! The plane descends even more now, and your view of what's to come turns from vision to reality.

The plane is arriving on time, and your purpose is on schedule to land momentarily. The seat belt sign has now been turned on; please prepare for landing!

Plus three minus eight

Experts projected that 80 percent of all plane crashes happen within the first three minutes of a flight or in the last eight minutes before landing. Candidly, landing is dangerous and overcoming landing issues is no easy feat.

Weight, speed, and landing gear all have landing requirements that are essential for a safe landing. You have to engage your systems and your speed in anticipation of the transition to touchdown.

Just as it was important to shed baggage for this flight, it's very important that an aircraft sheds weight along the journey. Because you have burned fuel along the way, your landing weight should be lower than your take-off weight. There is danger and much delay in unnecessary baggage and weight!

If you can't live longer, live deeper!

—Italian Proverb

The reality is that flying comes with risk and there will be planes that crash during landing. Tragically, planes filled with people have fallen from the sky into a thick flame of smoke. Whether from wind overtaking the aircraft, damage to the aircraft, electric failure, loss of control, error, or the unknown, they did not make it to their intended destination. This is a grim reality and a reminder for us to do everything in our power to be aligned with God on a daily basis.

We must be covered. We must pray.

I watched several documentaries about those who have passed in plane crashes. Collectively, the families who were most comforted talked about their loved ones living out their passion, the impact they had on others, and witnessing them live out their purpose. To live a life of passion and purpose before our final call is the ultimate goal. Death is no respecter of age, financial status, ethnicity, gender, or any demographic for that matter.

Nevertheless,

God is faithful when life isn't fair. We may never know why certain things happen, but we can anchor ourselves in what we know to be true: God's love.

Black box

The aircraft has a little black box that keeps a record of everything involving the plane's data and communication. It is also the most indestructible component of an aircraft. Similarly, in life, the way in which we live and the way in which we honored our calling, in combination with the legacy we leave behind, is the most everlasting thing we can gift others and ourselves.

What's in your black box?

"Purpose is an essential element of you. Purpose is what God put inside you that you're supposed to give to the world."

—Chadwick Boseman

Final approach

You are now ready to land on purpose! This is your final approach before you reach your destiny. The journey doesn't seem so long when your eyes can conceptualize the beauty of your new reality. Take inventory. The time is now, and your destiny is here.

Take a deep breath & appreciate the journey.

The journey is where you found yourself. The destiny is where you get to live out your best life and share your gifts with others.

Take a deep breath & appreciate the journey.

The journey is where you found your courage and created new possibilities beyond fear. You didn't give up, and you didn't lose faith.

Take a deep breath & appreciate the journey.

The journey is your evidence that God is up to something big in your life. This is only the beginning.

Are you ready to claim what is yours?

Destiny Touchdown

The wheels have touched down on the runway. Intention, influence, and favor meet a significant touch point: destiny. As a plane touches down on international soil, you have touched down on purpose soil. This is your place of more!

Millions Soil

Overflow Soil

Redemption Soil

Expansion Soil

MORE is now the anchorage for everything you stand for and everything you do! This soil, founded in grace, will enrich your faith, your commitment, your beliefs, your resilience, your relentlessness, your courage, your boldness, your authenticity, and your confidence in God's promises.

Godspeed

God. Speed. You.

My friend, the real journey is just beginning. May God's best for your life, the calling He placed in your heart, and the purpose He created you for be realized now.

Ladies and gentlemen, welcome to living your best life. The local time is NOW, and the temperature is a degree above your comfort level. The seat belt sign has been turned off, and it is safe for you to go forth and do extraordinary things. At this time, you may use your cellular devices. Please check around your seat for any personal belongings you may have brought on board with you, and please use caution when opening the overhead bins, as heavy articles may have shifted during the flight. As you depart the aircraft, please take note of the mini flip-book travel brochure filled with exciting information on how to LIVE ON PURPOSE. Be sure to make this the most remarkable experience! On behalf of Bella Layor Transformational Airlines, we thank you for taking this flight, and we look forward to servicing you again in the near future.

L.I.V.E   O.N   P.U.R.P.O.S.E!

Longevity for the Long Haul

Inner First-Class Experience

Vertical Vantage (perspective)

Expectations & Encounters

Operating Cost

No Smoking

Inside the Cabin

Positioned to Prevail

Understanding Your Airworthiness

Return on Investment

Passport Power

Only God Could have Orchestrated This

Stand by: I am Ready to be Used by God

Expand Your Vision Worldwide

Flight Segment 40
Longevity For The Long Haul

Your purposeful life is comprised of many moments, not just one. Don't stay stuck in a moment of regret. You have the power to navigate your path. When times get tough, look in the mirror and choose grace! Rise up stronger each time you feel defeated; you are a warrior! Take time to build up your stamina and take time to rest along the way. The marathon is underway.

Flight Segment 41
Inner First-Class Experience

One conduit between where you are and where you are going is your internal experience. It's easy to show compassion to others when it is clear they are in need, but don't forget to show that compassion, forgiveness, and patience to yourself.

You deserve the best life has to offer, but it starts with your inner world before it's deeply reflected, enjoyed, and appreciated outwardly.

Claim Inner Wisdom and Abundance

Claim Self Care and Positive Self Talk

Claim Peace and Joy

Claim Full Restoration

Claim Clarity and Truth

Claim Love and Beauty

Claim Transformation and Unwavering Faith

Claim Excellence and Wellbeing,

It's yours!

Flight Segment 42
Vertical Vantage

See the bigger picture.

How you see things from the ground will be very different from how you see things from the skies. Your perspective changes your reality and your understanding.

> "Your perspective will either become your prison or your passport."
>
> —Steven Furtick

Flight Segment 43
Expectations & Encounters

Anticipate a move of God on your life. You are His chosen one.

This is an unconditional kind of love

This is a forever kind of love

He adores you and wants you to be blessed in everything.

So, live in agreement with God's promises through your words and actions.

Take time to see God in everything. He is always there.

Flight Segment 44
Operating Cost

The road less traveled will cost you.

Discipline is the currency!

Discipline your thoughts.

Discipline with your time.

Discipline with your energy.

Discipline with your money.

Discipline to master self-control.

Discipline with your decisions.

Discipline with everything you consume.

No Excuses.

Start Now & Be Consistent

Flight Segment 45
No Smoking Inside The Cabin

Air ventilation is already limited onboard an aircraft.

Why stifle yourself or let others stifle you?

Smoke drifts everywhere!

Don't you dare be the one to sabotage your own wellbeing, and don't you dare surround yourself with toxic people. Their habits can contaminate the quality of your air.

Smoking is a hazard to your vision, your mind, and your health.

You need clear vision and good oxygen for the journey.

No more self-sabotage;

Sabotage self no more!

Flight Segment 46
Positioned To Prevail

Grace has been where you were, and grace goes before you.

You are positioned to overcome anything that comes your way!

Your problems are no match for your potential.

See opportunities at every peak and every valley.

Make progress the goal, not perfection.

You are favored for this!

Believe and know that everything is going to work out for your good.

Flight Segment 47
Understanding Your Airworthiness Through Grace

Every airplane isn't approved for the skies. Additionally, every airplane isn't approved for every flight. Similarly, there is something God approved you to do that only you can do! You have been chosen and purposed for your calling. No one can take that from you. You belong here. No matter how unworthy you may feel and no matter what has taken place in your past, God has certified you and given you the authority to take flight to your destiny!

Flight Segment 48
Return On Investment

An ROI can result in a negative return or a positive one, depending on performance.

Make sure you are investing wisely. By now, you know deep down what has yielded a good return in your life and what has yielded nothing or even what has depleted what you initially invested.

What is your biggest investment?

Where do you need to invest more?

What increases your purpose profit?

Flight Segment 49
Passport Power

When travelling outside familiar territory, you need a passport. This is a verification of your identity and confirmation of the access given to you. Travel to new horizons. Experience the array of beautiful sunsets across the globe. Share your smile and share your testimony. Give hope and leave with gratitude. And, when you journey back to the place you used to be, don't forget you will still need your passport.

Although your past may be a source of pain, you can return with purpose, sharing your light so that others too can see.

Flight Segment 50
Only God Could Have Orchestrated This

In a world where we try to control the outcomes of everything, there are things that only God can orchestrate. You have to trust Him in order to see. Our plans may be good, but His are far beyond our greatest imagination. Learn to trust Him. There are things that are not within your power to change.

Surrender

Your

Will

For

His

Flight Segment 51
Stand by: Ready to be Used by God

Standby is a process of waiting for an opportunity; it's not a guarantee, it's a possibility.

Always prepare to be used by God. There is no moment too small or great, God can use you if you are willing and ready. Aside from your larger purpose, you will be afforded opportunities to fill gaps that have gone unoccupied. It could be a kind word spoken or a random act of kindness.

Whatever God tells you, great or small, do it and stand by to witness His goodness and the blessings that follow.

When the Lord calls your name, boldly answer!

Flight Segment 52
Expand Your Vision Worldwide

God gave me a vision during the lowest point in my life. That vision was a forecast of my healed self. Within the vision, I overcame all trauma from my past and was sharing hope and healing with many others from a stage. I showed evidence of inner peace and inner grit as I talked on stage. The vision ended with me walking down a set of stairs, hugging and embracing those who were hurting but felt heard and inspired to heal. It was powerful to witness from a place of victimhood and be the woman in the vision at the same time. From that moment forward, I was on a quest to heal, rebuild, and transform my life. That vision was one key to my healing. One that I now share with the world.

Your freedom is meant to free many others.

Life is a journey; enjoy the flight!

To most people, the sky is the limit.

To others, the sky is home.

—Unknown author

And to my father, who never clipped my wings. You lifted my head, reminded me I was made to soar, and always poured life into my dreams.

Thank you for being. Thank you for always uplifting me. I love you and thank God for you always!

www.ingramcontent.com/pod-product-compliance
Lightning Source LLC
Chambersburg PA
CBHW050726010526
44107CB00009B/753